WITHDRAWN
WORN, SOILED, OBSOLETE

Luxe Knits

Luxe Knits

Couture Designs to Knit & Crochet

Laura Zukaite

Photography by Cathrine Westergaard

LARK BOOKS

A Division of Sterling Publishing Co., Inc.
New York / London

SENIOR EDITOR
Valerie Shrader

EDITOR
Linda Kopp

ART DIRECTOR
Dana Irwin

ART PRODUCTION
Carol Morse

TECHNICAL EDITOR
Amy Polcyn

EDITORIAL ASSISTANCE
Amanda Carestio

FIGURATIVE ILLUSTRATOR
Laura Zukaite

SCHEMATICS ILLUSTRATOR
Orrin Lundgren

PHOTOGRAPHER
Cathrine Westergaard

COVER DESIGNER
woolypear

Library of Congress Cataloging-in-Publication Data

Zukaite, Laura.
  Luxe Knits : couture designs to knit & crochet / Laura Zukaite. -- 1st ed.
     p. cm.
  Includes index.
  ISBN 978-1-60059-283-6 (hc-plc with jacket : alk. paper)
  1. Knitting--Patterns. 2. Crocheting--Patterns. I. Title.
  TT825.Z85 2009
  746.43'2041--dc22

                          2008050623

10 9 8 7 6 5 4 3 2 1

First Edition

Published by Lark Books, A Division of
Sterling Publishing Co., Inc.
387 Park Avenue South, New York, NY 10016

Text © 2009, Laura Zukaite
Figurative Illustrations © 2009, Laura Zukaite
Photography © 2009, Lark Books,
a Division of Sterling Publishing Co., Inc., unless otherwise specified
Schematic Illustrations © 2009, Lark Books, a Division of Sterling Publishing Co.

Distributed in Canada by Sterling Publishing,
c/o Canadian Manda Group, 165 Dufferin Street
Toronto, Ontario, Canada M6K 3H6

Distributed in the United Kingdom by GMC Distribution Services,
Castle Place, 166 High Street, Lewes, East Sussex, England BN7 1XU

Distributed in Australia by Capricorn Link (Australia) Pty Ltd.,
P.O. Box 704, Windsor, NSW 2756 Australia

If you have questions or comments about this book, please contact:
Lark Books
67 Broadway
Asheville, NC 28801
828-253-0467

Manufactured in China

ISBN 13: 978-1-60059-283-6

For information about custom editions, special sales, premium and corporate purchases, please
contact Sterling Special Sales Department at 800-805-5489 or specialsales@sterlingpub.com.

contents

Introduction

Instead of writing the typical knitting book that features only projects, I set out to share my inspiration and design process with you so you have a greater understanding of how fashion and function interact and change during the creation of a garment. As a young designer, I strongly believe in universal and timeless fashion, and what challenges me is finding a way to make an object both pleasing to the eye *and* practical. You'll discover that designing knitwear involves a bit of creative problem solving; I always keep function in mind but I also want the garments to reflect my own beliefs about style. Sometimes this requires a compromise between the two. So in *Luxe Knits* I wanted to show how design evolves: from an initial inspiration to an interpretation of technique; from technique to fashion sketches; and from sketches to an actual garment.

INSPIRATION AND INTERPRETATION

Each designer expresses his or her vision through various elements, including shape, color, drape, and texture. Sometimes everyday objects serve as inspiration, and these objects are then interpreted through design. Many of the projects in this book began this way; for example, the texture of frost on a window was the basis for the Tonal Transitions chapter, while the geometric patterns found in nature were translated into some of the Herringbone Evolution garments. This quote from *The Picture of Dorian Gray* by Oscar Wilde best describes my own design philosophy: "A dream of form in days of thought." What this means to me is that I design to discover a form—a sweater or a skirt or a scarf—that stops the mind for a second and lets it enjoy a moment of beauty and visual satisfaction.

I believe in universal and timeless fashion

A beautifully designed object rarely displays all these little discoveries inherent in the creative process. To me, initial inspiration is where it all begins: it plays such a major role that it determines the shapes, textures, and even colors of my design. Then interpretation comes into play: sometimes a design strays so far from the initial source of ideas that the inspiration gets lost in the piece, yet other times it is almost literal.

EVOLUTION AND EXPERIMENTATION

Let's take one of the most abstract interpretations as an example of how design evolves: the Folding Obsession projects. In this chapter the relation to the initial inspiration of vertical and horizontal lines is not easy to figure out from the first glance. When I started working on this idea, I knew I wanted a very simple texture and clear lines, which is why I chose to work with stockinette stitch. When playing with it, I discovered that a folded fabric creates very beautiful soft lines. Then one line followed the other, and soon I had in my hand a three-dimensional linear pattern. I started incorporating different fibers, weights, textures, and colors. I began designing garments only after I had explored all the possibilities of the technique.

I usually have a few ideas when I start sketching, but once I begin to put them on paper, new ideas spring forth—at the end I have hundreds of little sketches to pick from. Choosing the ones to execute is the hardest part, since all the sketches become my favorites by the time they are done! I try to be diverse with my choices, so for Folding Obsession I picked a cardigan, a shrug, a hat, and a pair of gloves—a couple of garments and a couple of accessories.

CONSTRUCTION AND COMPROMISE

After I choose the pieces, I begin to create each one. Designing is really a very long process, since after you actually start making a garment you may realize that it's impossible to achieve what you had put down on paper. That's where my favorite part of design—problem solving—comes in. The Shawl Sweater (page 18) is a good example; I initially envisioned this piece done all in one fiber. However, after I started knitting it I realized that the shawl collar was going to be too heavy to drape properly, so I combined a lace-weight mohair in between the folds to achieve the look I wanted. Ultimately, the design process is all about smart solutions and compromises, and it is much more complex than it might seem from just looking at a finished piece.

EXECUTION AND ENCOURAGEMENT

Most of the projects in *Luxe Knits* came from the sketchbook I created during my senior year at Parsons The New School for Design. The eight chapters in this book are based on re-interpretations of traditional stitch patterns, and each illustrates some new and unique ways that well-known and well-loved stitches can be used. Often these patterns twist and turn and change into something new, or they develop an exciting form or detail. Three projects from the Honeycomb Adaptations chapter illustrate this dynamic: shaping within the pattern achieved a seamless fitted waistline in the Peplum Cardigan (page 134); the pattern was turned upside-down and draped over the shoulders in the Fitted Blouse (page 126); and then finally decreasing within the stitch pattern created the shape of the Scallop Purse (page 130). In the other chapters you'll also discover something new and interesting about smocking stitch, herringbone pattern, butterfly stitch, cables, and of course stockinette stitch. The projects themselves begin on page 10, and the schematics for all the designs are grouped together on pages 141-143.

Because we all form long-term relationships with our knitting projects, my wish is that this book will give you some tools to use as you spend many enjoyable hours with your own work. I hope a peek into my design process will inspire and challenge you to begin your own experimentation with different stitches, textures, and color work.

folding

CHAPTER 1

obsession

The following four projects take a simple stockinette stitch and make it three-dimensional by creating folds that are then incorporated into the designs in unique and intriguing ways. There's so much you can do by simply folding already knitted stockinette fabric and knitting it together with the stitches in the back—the results can be dense and chunky, delicate and lacy, or fun and colorful.

long gloves

Extended proportions
are eternally elegant and in
vogue. Luxurious cashmere yarn
caresses, and a little folded trim
provides textural interest.

Artyarns Cashmere 3 (100% cashmere; 1.75oz/50g = 170yd/153m): 2 skeins, color cream #250—approx 340yd/306m of light worsted weight yarn (3)

Knitting needles: 3.75mm (size 5 U.S.) double-pointed needles *or size to obtain gauge*

Stitch markers

Scrap yarn in contrast color

⅛" (3mm) leather lacing, 1yd/1m (optional)

Tapestry needle

SKILL LEVEL
Intermediate

SIZE
Women's average

FINISHED
MEASUREMENTS
**Cuff circumference:
8"/20.5cm**

GAUGE

23 sts and 28 rows = 4"/10cm in St st

Always take time to check your gauge.

instructions

GLOVES (MAKE 2)

CO 46 sts. PM and join in a round, being careful not to twist the sts.

Fold Trim:

Knit for 6 rounds.

Next round (fold round): Lift first CO st from back and place on left needle, knit tog with first st of round; *lift next CO st from back and place on left needle, knit tog with next st; rep from * around (fold 1). **Continue in St st for 5 more rounds; rep fold round, but this time pick up the corresponding purl st 5 rounds below (fold 2).

Rep from ** twice more.

Work even in St st for 2"/5 cm more.

Next (dec) round: Knit to 18 sts before marker, k2tog, k18 sts, PM, ssk—44 sts.

Rep dec round on every following 6th round 3 times—38 sts.

Then work even until piece measures 8"/21cm from beg.

THUMB GUSSET SHAPING:

Work to 2nd marker, M1, k1, M1, PM (marker #3).

Inc 1 st after the 2nd and before the 3rd markers on every other round until there are 19 sts between the markers.

Slip these 19 sts on a piece of waste yarn for thumb.

On the next round, CO 2 sts over the gap at the thumb and join in a round for the palm, PM for new beg of round.

Work these 39 sts even for 1"/2.5cm, then divide for fingers.

INDEX SHAPING:

Knit to marker, k4, place last 11 sts that were worked on double-pointed needles, CO 3 more sts and join in a round (put remaining 28 sts on a piece of waste yarn).

Knit these 14 sts until finger measures 1¾"/4.5cm.

Next round: [Sl 1, k2tog, psso, k4] twice—10 sts.

Knit 1 round.

Next round: [Sl 1, k2tog, psso, k2] twice—6 sts.

Cut yarn and slip yarn through remaining sts, fasten off.

MIDDLE FINGER:

Slip next 5 palm sts on needles, CO 1 st, slip 5 corresponding back of hand sts on needles, pick up and knit 3 sts from the base of the CO sts of the index finger (14 sts total), PM and join in a round. Work as for index finger.

RING FINGER:

Work as for middle finger.

PINKY:

Slip rem 8 sts from waste yarn on needles, pick up and knit 3 sts from the base of the CO sts of the ring finger (11 sts total), PM and join in a round.

Knit these 11 sts until finger measures 1¼"/3cm.

Next round: Sl 1, k2tog, psso, k3, sl 1, k2tog, psso, k2—7 sts.

Next round: Sl 1, k2tog, psso, k1, sl 1, k2tog, psso—3 sts.

Cut yarn and slip yarn through remaining sts, fasten off.

THUMB:

Slip 19 thumb sts to needles, pick up and knit 2 sts from side of palm (21 sts total), PM for new beg of round.

Knit 1 round.

Next round: [Sl 1, k2tog, psso, k7] twice, k1—17 sts.

Work 4 more rounds even, then start top shaping:

Next round: [Sl 1, k2tog, psso, k5] twice, k1—13 sts.

Knit 1 round.

Next round: [Sl 1, k2tog, psso, k3] twice, k1—9 sts.

Knit 1 round.

Next round: [Sl 1, k2tog, psso, k1] twice, k1—5 sts.

Cut yarn and slip through remaining sts, fasten off.

FINISHING

Weave in ends. If desired, weave leather lace as shown to add another design element to the glove, reversing on the other glove.

love knitted accessories—they can really complete an outfit. In this case, I was going for a more glamorous look: an elongated shape with a touch of folded trim at the cuff.

Think of this hat as a blank canvas.
Experiment and work it up using
multiple yarns to make a fresh,
original statement.

folded hat

SKILL LEVEL
Intermediate

SIZE
Women's

FINISHED MEASUREMENTS
Head circumference: 21"/53.5cm

YOU WILL NEED

Artyarns Silk Mohair Glitter (60% super kid mohair, 40% silk; 0.88oz/25g = 312yd/281m): (A) 1 skein, color natural/gold; (F) 1 skein, color rose/silver; (K) 1 skein, color multi/gold—approx 936yd/842m of lace weight yarn 🄋

Artyarns Silk Mohair (60% super kid mohair, 40% silk; 0.88oz/25g = 312yd/281m): 1 skein, color peach #128—approx 312yd/281m of lace weight yarn 🄋 (D)

Artyarns Regal Silk (100% silk; 1.75oz/50g = 163yd/147m): (B) 1 skein, color bronze #261; (C) 1 skein, color light peach #253; (H) 1 skein, color light pink #215; (L) 1 skein, color multi; (M) 1 skein, color green #233—approx 815yd/734m of light worsted weight yarn 🄌

Artyarns Ultramerino 6 (100% merino wool; 3.5oz/100g = 274yd/247m): (E) 1 skein, color dark peach #221; (J) 1 skein, color variegated brown #137—approx 548yd/493m of light worsted weight yarn 🄌

Artyarns Cashmere 3 (100% cashmere; 1.75oz/50g = 170yd/153m): (G) 1 skein, color rose #262, (I) 1 skein, color cream #250—approx 340yd/306m of light worsted weight yarn 🄌

NOTE: Only partial balls of each color are required for this project.

Knitting needles: 4mm (size 6 U.S.) 16"/40.5cm circular needle and double-pointed needles *or size to obtain gauge*

Stitch marker

Tapestry needle

21 sts = 4"/10cm in St st using heavier yarn

Always take time to check your gauge.

instructions

HAT

Using A (lighter weight yarn) and circular needle, CO 96 sts.

PM and join in a round, being careful not to twist the sts.

FOLD PATTERN 1:

Work 5 rounds in St st.

Round 6: Lift first CO st from back and place on left needle, knit tog with first st of round, *lift next CO st from back and place on left needle, knit tog with next st; rep from * around (fold created).

Space Between Folds:

With B, work in St st for 6 rounds (first pattern set completed).

START FOLD PATTERN II:

With A, work 5 rounds in St st.

Round 6: Pick up st from back 5 rounds below and place on left needle, knit tog with first st of round, *lift next st from back 5 rounds below and place on left needle, knit tog with next st; rep from * around (fold created).

Space Between Folds:

With C, work in St st for 6 rounds (second pattern set completed).

Repeat Fold Pattern II and Space Between Folds 3 more times using colors as follows:

Pattern repeat 3: D/E

Pattern repeat 4: F/G

Pattern repeat 5: F/H

Crown shaping (change to double-pointed needles when needed):

Pattern repeat 6: D/I

With D, *k10, k2tog, rep from * around—88 sts.

Work 4 rounds in St st.

Round 6: Rep Round 6 of Fold Pattern II.

Space Between Folds:

With I, work 1 round in St st.

Round 2: *K9, k2tog; rep from * around—80 sts.

Rounds 3 & 5: Knit.

Round 4: *K8, k2tog; rep from * around—72 sts.

Pattern repeat 7: F/J

With F, work 5 rounds in St st.

Round 6: Rep round 6 of Fold Pattern II.

Space Between Folds:

With J, work 1 round in St st.

Round 2: *K7, k2tog; rep from * around—64 sts.

Rounds 3 & 5: Knit.

Round 4: *K6, k2tog; rep from * around—56 sts.

Pattern repeat 8: K/L

With K, *k5, k2tog; rep from * around—48 sts.

Work 4 rounds in St st.

Round 6: Rep round 6 of Fold Pattern II.

Space Between Folds:

With L, work 1 round in St st.

Round 2: *K4, k2tog; rep from * around—40 sts.

Rounds 3 & 5: Knit.

Round 4: *K3, k2tog; rep from * around—32 sts.

Pattern repeat 9: K/M

With F, work 5 rounds in St st.

Round 6: Rep round 6 of Fold Pattern II.

Space Between Folds:

With M, work 1 round in St st.

Round 2: *K2, k2tog; rep from * around—24 sts.

Rounds 3, 5, & 7: Knit.

Round 4: *K1, k2tog; rep from * around—16 sts.

Round 6: *K2tog; rep from * around—8 sts.

Cut a long tail and slip 8 live sts through. Fasten off.

FINISHING

Weave in ends. Block to finished size.

I wanted to create a piece that would represent the many ways the folding technique can be used—including color. The technique is best show-cased in a small piece like a hat where the folds and color work don't overwhelm.

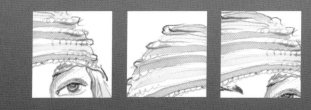

shawl sweater

The combination of light and heavy fibers creates the graceful draping effect for this collar, which can be tied or wrapped to suit multiple tastes.

Artyarns Silk Rhapsody (100% silk core, wrapped in 70% mohair/30% silk; 3.5oz/100g = 260yd/234m): (A) 5 (6, 6) skeins, color cream #250; (B) 2 skeins, color rose natural #137— approx 1820 (2080, 2080) yd/1638 (1872, 1872)m of worsted weight yarn (4)

Artyarns Silk Mohair (60% super kid mohair, 40% silk; 0.88oz/25g = 312yd/281m): 2 skeins, color cream #250—approx 624yd/562m of lace weight yarn (0) (C)

Knitting needles: 4.5mm (size 7 U.S.) 32"/81cm circular needles and 8mm (size 11 U.S.) 32"/81cm circular needles *or size to obtain gauge*

Stitch markers

Stitch holders

Tapestry needle

SKILL LEVEL
Intermediate

SIZE
Women's S (M, L)

FINISHED
MEASUREMENTS
Bust: 34 (38, 42)"/86.5 (96.5, 107)cm

Length: 22½ (23, 24)"/57 (58, 61)cm

GAUGE

18 sts and 28 rows = 4"/10cm in St st using heavier yarn and smaller needles

Always take time to check your gauge.

PATTERN STITCH

Border Ridge:

Beginning with a WS row, work 5 rows in St st, slipping the 1st st of each row.

Next row (RS): Fold work to WS, forming a tube; *(insert right needle in first st on left needle, then in corresponding st on CO edge, knit these 2 sts tog); rep from * to end (first ridge complete).

****Starting with WS row, work 5 rows in St st.

Next row (RS): Fold work to WS, forming a tube; *(insert right needle in st on needle, then in corresponding st on row 5 rows down, knit these 2 sts tog); rep from * to end (ridge complete).

Rep from ** for pattern.

instructions

BODY

NOTE: The body is worked in one piece.

Using A and smaller needles, CO 159 (179, 199) sts.

Work the bottom hem in Border Ridge pattern, making a total of 4 ridges.

Work in St st for 21 rows.

Next (dec) row (RS): Work 39 (46, 53) sts, PM, sl 1, k2tog, psso; knit 75 (81, 87) more sts, sl 1, k2tog, psso, PM, knit remaining 39 (46, 53) sts—155 (175, 195) sts.

Work even for 5 (7, 7) more rows.

WAIST SHAPING

Next (dec) row (RS): Work to 1 st before the 1st marker, move marker, sl 1, k2tog, psso; knit to 1 st before the 2nd marker, move marker, sl 1, k2tog, psso, knit remaining sts—151 (171, 191) sts.

Work even for 5 (5, 7) more rows.

Rep last dec row once more—147 (167, 187) sts.

Work even for 5 more rows.

Rep last dec row once more—143 (163, 183) sts.

Work even for 1 more row.

Rep last dec row once more—139 (159, 179) sts.

Work even for 5 (7, 7) more rows.

Next (inc) row (RS): Sl 1, k2tog, work to the 1st marker, M1, k1, M1; knit to 1 st before the 2nd marker, M1, k1, M1, knit remaining sts, ssk, k1—141 (161, 181) sts.

Work even for 7 (7, 9) more rows.

Rep inc row once more—143 (163, 183) sts.

Work even for 7 more rows.

Rep inc row once more—145 (165, 185) sts.

Work even for 7 more rows.

*Rep inc row once more—147 (167, 187) sts.

Work even for 4 more rows.

Rep from * twice more—151 (171, 191) sts.

Work even until piece measures 15 (15½, 16)"/38 (39.5, 41)cm from beg, ending with a WS row.

ARMHOLE AND NECK/PLACKET SHAPING

Next row (RS): Sl 1, k2tog, work to 3 sts before the marker (right front), BO next 6 sts, knit to 3 sts before the 2nd marker (back), BO next 6 sts, work to last 3 sts, ssk, k1 (left front). You will have 31/75/31 sts remaining. Turn and work left front only as follows:

LEFT FRONT:

Row 1 (WS): Work to last 2 sts, p2tog.

Row 2 (RS): BO 3 sts, knit to end.

Rep rows 1 and 2, 0 (1, 2) times more.

Next row (WS): Work to last 2 sts, p2tog.

Next row: BO 1 st, knit to last 3 sts, ssk, k1.

Next row: Work to last 2 sts, p2tog.

Work even for 8 rows.

Next row (RS): Work to last 3 sts, ssk, k1—22 (25, 28) sts.

Work even until armhole measures 7½ (7½, 8)"/19 (19, 20.5)cm. Place remaining sts on a holder.

RIGHT FRONT:

Join yarn on RS and work as for Left Front, reversing shaping.

BACK

Join yarn on RS.

Row 1 (RS): K2tog, work to last 2 sts, ssk.

Row 2: BO 3 sts, work to last 2 sts, p2tog.

Row 3: BO 3 sts, work to last 2 sts, ssk.

Rep rows 2 and 3, 0 (1, 2) times more.

Next row (WS): BO 1 st, work to last 2 sts, p2tog.

Next row: BO 1 st, work to last 2 sts, ssk.

Work even for 9 rows.

Next row (RS): K2tog, work to last 2 sts, ssk. 59 (55, 53) sts left.

Work even until armhole measures 7½ (7½, 8)"/19 (19, 20.5)cm. Place 22 (25, 28) shoulder sts from each side on holders, BO rem sts.

SLEEVES (MAKE 2)

Using A and smaller needles, CO 38 (40, 42) sts.

Work in Border Ridge pattern for 4 ridges.

Work in St st for ½"/1.5cm.

Inc 1 st at beg and end of every 8th row 6 (7, 7) times—50 (54, 56) sts.

Inc 1 st at the beg and end of every 12th row 5 times—60 (64, 66) sts.

Work even until sleeve measures 20 (20½, 21)"/51 (52, 53.5)cm.

CAP SHAPING:

Rows 1 (RS) & 2: BO 3 sts, work to end.

Rows 3 & 4: BO 2 sts, work to last 2 sts, k2tog.

Rows 5 & 6: BO 1 st, work till the last 2 sts, k2tog—44 (48, 50) sts.

Dec 1 st at beg and end of every 6th RS row once—42 (46, 48) sts.

Dec 1 st at beg and end of row every 4th row 5 times—32 (36, 38) sts.

Work even for 2 more rows.

BO 1 st at beg of the following 2 (4, 4) rows—30 (32, 34) sts.

BO 2 sts at beg of the following 4 rows—22 (24, 26) sts.

BO 3 sts at the beg of next 4 rows—10 (12, 14) sts.

BO.

COLLAR

FOLD:

With 2 strands of B held double and larger needles, CO 270 (274, 278) sts.

FIRST SET OF FOLDS:

Rows 1, 3, & 5 (RS): Knit.

Rows 2, 4, & 6: Purl.

Change to C.

Row 7 (RS): *Sl 1, pick up a corresponding st from back of work from 6 rows below and knit tog; rep from * to end (fold complete).

Rows 8–14: Using 1 strand of A, work in St st.

Rep First Set of Folds once.

SECOND SET OF FOLDS:

Change to 2 strands of B and work fold as before.

Next 7 rows: Rep rows 8–14 as before, using 2 strands of C.

Rep First Set of Folds twice more.

Rep First Set of Folds once more, BO after Row 7.

FINISHING

Join shoulder seams with 3-needle BO. Attach sleeves, and sew sleeve seams.

Center the cast-on row of the collar on the center back and attach down the back neck and front side openings, leaving ends of the collar unattached. Weave in ends.

this sweater came straight from my college thesis collection. To me, it represents both form and function in one garment. The exaggerated collar shape allows the sweater to be worn in multiple ways.

a folding pattern establishes dimension in this ultra-mod shrug, while the varied yarn fibers and weights suggest textural depth.

cinched shrug

YOU WILL NEED

Jade Sapphire Maju Silk (100% silk; 1.75oz/50g = 85yd/77m): 3 skeins, color silver fern #34—approx 255yd/230m of worsted weight yarn (4) (A)

Jade Sapphire 4-ply Mongolian Cashmere (100% cashmere; 1.9oz/55g = 200yd/180m): 1 skein, color silver fern #34—approx 200yd/180m of sport weight yarn (2) (B)

Jade Sapphire 2-ply Mongolian Cashmere (100% cashmere; 1.9oz/55g = 400yd/360m): 1 skein, color silver fern #34—approx 400yd/360m of fingering weight yarn (1) (C)

Knitting needles: 6mm (size 10 U.S.) *or size to obtain gauge*

Tapestry needle

SKILL LEVEL
Intermediate

SIZE
Women's S (M, L)

FINISHED MEASUREMENTS
Upper arm circumference: 11 (13, 15)"/28 (33, 38)cm

Length: 50 (50½, 53)"/127 (128, 135) cm, cuff to cuff

GAUGE

16 sts and 18 rows = 4"/10cm in St st using heavier yarn

Always take time to check your gauge.

PATTERN STITCH

Cuff Ridge:

Beginning with a WS row, work 5 rows in St st, slipping the 1st st of each row.

Next row (RS): Fold work to WS, forming a tube; *(insert right needle in first st on left needle, then in corresponding st on CO edge, knit these 2 sts tog); rep from * to end (first ridge complete).

**Starting with WS row, work 5 rows in St st.

Next row (RS): Fold work to WS, forming a tube; *(insert right needle in st on needle, then in corresponding st on row 5 rows down, knit these 2 sts tog); rep from * to end (ridge complete).

Rep from ** for pattern.

instructions

SHRUG

With A (heavier weight yarn), CO 36 (42, 48) sts.

Work in Cuff Ridge pattern for 9 (10, 10) ridges.

Change to C (lightest weight yarn) on last RS row of ridge pattern and use to join last fold.

Next (inc) row (WS): Sl 1, *p2, M1; rep from * to last st, p1—53 (62, 71) sts.

Work in C in St st for 7 rows.

First Set of Folds:

Change to A and work fold as follows:

Rows 1, 3, & 5 (RS): Knit.

Rows 2, 4, & 6: Purl.

Change to C.

Row 7 (RS): *Sl 1, pick up a corresponding st from back of work from 6 rows below and knit tog; rep from * to end (fold complete).

Rows 8–14: Using C, work in St st.

Rep First Set of Folds once.

Second Set of Folds:

Change to A and work fold as before.

Next 7 rows: Rep rows 8–14 as before, using B (medium weight yarn).

Rep rows 1–14, 18 (18, 19) times more.

Rep the First Set of Folds twice.

Work First Set of Folds once more, except work last row as follows:

Row 14: P1, *(p2tog, p1); rep from * to last st, p1—36 (42, 48) sts.

Using A, work in Cuff Ridge pattern for 9 (10, 10) ridges. BO on the folding row of ridge 9 (10, 10).

FINISHING

Fold shrug in half, and seam from cuffs to approx 16¾ (17½, 18)"/42.5 (44.5, 46)cm in from ends on each side, leaving center open. Weave in ends.

When I started working on this idea, I knew I wanted a very simple texture and clear lines so I chose to work with the stockinette stitch. While playing with the stitch, I discovered a folded fabric that creates very beautiful, soft lines. One pattern repeat followed another, and before I knew it, I was holding a three-dimensional linear pattern.

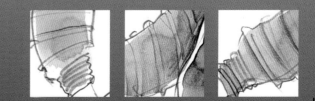

smocking stitch

CHAPTER 2

transformations

Inspired by the beauty of African textiles, I reinterpreted the old-fashioned smocking stitch in this chapter, revealing an entirely new look in texture and color work. These two very different projects present an exciting way of transforming this stitch into fresh design possibilities.

While the smocking stitch creates a beautiful fitted bodice, the rest of the silhouette is loose and free.

summer dress

SKILL LEVEL
Experienced

SIZE
Women's XS (S)

FINISHED MEASUREMENTS
Bust: 28 (34)"/71 (86.5)cm

Length: 31 (32½)"/79 (83)cm

YOU WILL NEED

Claudia Handpainted Linen (100% linen; 3.5oz/100g = 270yd/243m): 2 skeins, color natural—approx 540yd/486m of sport weight yarn (2) (A)

Claudia Handpainted Silk Lace (100% silk; 3.5oz/100g = 1100yd/990m): 1 skein, color marigold—approx 1100yd/990m of lace weight yarn (0) (B)

Claudia Handpainted Linen Lace (100% linen; 3.5oz/100g = 540yd/486m): (C) 1 skein, color honey; (D) 1 skein, color woodland moss; (E) 1 skein, color chocolate—approx 1620yd/1458m of fingering weight yarn (1)

Knitting needles: 4mm (size 6 U.S.) 24"/61cm circular needle *or size to obtain gauge*

Crochet hook: 3.25mm (size D U.S.)

Cable needle

Stitch markers

Tapestry needle

my

initial inspiration came from Richard Avedon photographs that had a little touch of Africa in them. For this dress I wanted something that encompassed the feel of the photos: very light, earthy, and natural looking, but at the same time fashionable. Hand-painted linen, silk yarns, and a bit of time were the solution.

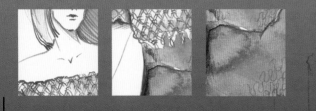

GAUGE

27 sts and 38 rows = 4"/10cm in St st using E

30 sts and 40 rows = 4"/10cm in Smocking Rib using A

Always take time to check your gauge.

SPECIAL ABBREVIATIONS

TW 3L: Sl 2 sts to cn and hold to front of work, (with B) p1, (with A) k2 from cn.

TW 3R: Sl 1 st to cn and hold to back of work, (with A) k2, (with B) p1 from cn.

TW 2L: Sl 1 st to cn and hold to front of work, (with B) p1, (with A) k1 from cn.

TW 2R: Sl 1 st to cn and hold to back of work, (with A) k1, (with B) p1 from cn.

PATTERN STITCHES

Smocking Rib in the Round (multiple of 8 sts):

Rounds 1, 2, 3, 5, 6, 7: *K2, p2; rep from * around.

Round 4: *Insert right needle between 6th and 7th st on left needle, wrap yarn around needle and pull up a loop, place loop on end of left needle (beside next st to be worked), k2tog (loop and 1st stitch), k1, p2, k2, p2; rep from * around.

Round 8: K2, p2, *insert right needle between 6th and 7th st on left needle and work as before, k2tog, k1, p2, k2, p2; rep from * to last 4 sts, insert needle after 1st 2 knit sts of next round (leave marker in place), wrap yarn and pull up a loop as before, k2tog, k1, p2.

Rep rounds 1–8 for pattern.

Smocking-to-Reverse Stockinette Transition:

NOTE: Carry both colors of yarn in back of work.

Rounds 1, 2, & 3: *(With A) k2, p2, k2, (with B) p2; rep from * around.

Round 4: *(With A) insert right needle from front to back between 6th and 7th sts on left needle and draw a loop through; slip this loop onto left needle and knit it tog with the 1st st on the same needle; k1, p2, k2, (with B) p2; rep from * around.

Round 5: Rep round 1.

Round 6: *(With A/B) TW 3R, TW 3L, (with B) p2; rep from * around.

Round 7: *(With A) k2, (with B) p2; rep from * around.

Round 8: *(With A/B) TW 2R, p2, TW 2L, p2; rep from * around.

Round 9 (Change to B completely): *K2tog, p6; rep from * around.

NOTE: Dress is worked top down. The upper body is worked in a round and then divided for front and back.

----

instructions

DRESS

Using A, CO 320 (352) sts. PM and join in a round, being careful not to twist the sts. Work in Smocking Rib pattern for 3 (3¼)"/8 (8) cm.

Divide for underarms:

Next round: BO 72 (72) sts, work next 88 (104) sts in pattern, BO next 72 (72) sts, work remaining 88 (104) sts in pattern.

Next round: CO 24 (24) sts over gap, continue working 88 (104) sts in pattern, CO 24 (24) sts over gap, work remaining 88 (104) sts in pattern—224 (256) sts.

Continue to work in the round in pattern until piece measures 4 (4½)"/10 (11.5)cm, ending with round 8.

NOTE: B is worked with 2 strands held double.

Next 9 rounds: Work Smocking-to-Reverse Stockinette Transition—196 (224) sts.

On the next row, mark the center of the underarms and divide evenly for front and back—98 (112) sts for each side.

Work front and back separately (and the same) in rows from this point on.

Using B, work in Rev St st for ½ (½)"/1.5 (1.5)cm. On last row, dec 7 (5) sts evenly across—91 (107) sts.

Then join C at each end of the panel as follows:

Row 1 (RS): (With C) sl 1, k2, PM, (with B) p85 (101), PM, k3.

Use C on the outside of markers, and B on the inside of markers.

Row 2: (With C) sl 1, M1, purl to 1 st after the 1st marker, move marker, (with B) knit to 1 st before the 2nd marker, move marker, (with C) purl to last st, M1, p1—93 (109) sts.

Row 3: (With C) sl 1, knit to 2 sts after the 1st marker, move marker, (with B) purl to 2 sts before the marker, move marker, (with C) knit remaining sts.

Row 4 (WS): Sl 1, purl to 1 st after the 1st marker, move marker, knit to 1 st before the 2nd marker, move marker, purl to end.

Row 5 (and every RS row): Rep row 3.

Rep rows 2-5 until there are 101 (117) sts on the needle, then rep same rows without working increases until there is 1 st left between markers. Change to C completely.

Work in St st for 32 (34) rows, inc 1 st at each end of every 4th row 5 times—111 (127) sts.

Add D and work same way as previously when adding C, but in reverse stitches (work St st in place of rev St st, and rev St st in place of St st).

Row 1: (With D) sl 1, p2, PM, (with C) knit to last 3 sts, PM, (with D) p3.

Work rows 2-5, but knit where previously purled and purl where previously knitted until there are 125 (141) sts on the needle, then rep same rows without working increases until there is 1 st left between markers. Change to D completely. Work in rev St st for 36 (38) rows, inc 1 st at each end of every 4th row 5 times—135 (151) sts.

Add E and work same way as previously when adding C.

Row 1: (With E) sl 1, k2, PM, (with D) purl to last 3 sts, PM, (with E) k3.

Work rows 2-5 until there are 145 (161) sts on the needle, then rep same rows without working increases until there is 1 st left between markers. Change to E completely. Work in rev St st for 24 (28) rows, increasing 1 st at each end of every foll 6th row 3 times—151 (167) sts.

Work in St st until dress measures 23½ (24½)"/59.5 (62)cm from underarms.

Work in garter stitch for ½ (½)"/1.5 (1.5)cm (4 more rows).

BO.

FINISHING

Sew the side seams using a matching color.

With A and crochet hook, sc along the top edge of each armhole. Weave in ends.

smocking pullover

The transition from smocking rib stitch in worsted weight yarn into reverse stockinette in a lighter yarn renders a smooth, sleek outline.

22 sts and 24 rows = 4"/10cm in Smocking Rib using A

20 sts and 24 rows = 4"/10cm in St st using B

Always take time to check your gauge.

SPECIAL ABBREVIATION

TW 3L: Sl 2 sts to cn and hold to front of work, (with B) p1, (with A) k2 from cn.

TW 3R: Sl 1 st to cn and hold to back of work, (with A) k2, (with B) p1 from cn.

TW 2L: Sl 1 st to cn and hold to front of work, (with B) p1, (with A) k1 from cn.

TW 2R: Sl 1 st to cn and hold to back of work, (with A) k1, (with B) p1 from cn.

PATTERN STITCH

Smocking Rib (multiple of 8+2 sts):

Rows 1 and 3 (WS): Sl 1, *k2, p2; rep from * to last st, k1.

Row 2: Sl 1,*k2, p2; rep from * to last st, k1.

Row 4: Sl 1, * insert right needle from front to back between 6th and 7th sts on left needle and draw a loop through; sl this loop onto left needle and knit it tog with the 1st st on the same needle; k1, p2, k2, p2; rep from * to last st, k1.

Rows 5 and 7: Rep rows 1 & 3.

Row 6: Rep row 2.

Row 8: Sl 1, k2, p2, * draw a loop from between 6th and 7th sts as before and knit it tog with 1st st, k1, p2, k2, p2; rep from *, end k2, p2, k1.

Rep rows 1–8 for pattern.

Smocking-to-Reverse Stockinette Transition:

NOTE: Carry both colors of yarn in back of work.

YOU WILL NEED

Blue Sky Alpacas Worsted Hand Dyes (50% alpaca, 50% merino wool; 3.5oz/100g = 100yd/90m): 4 skeins, color tan #2009—approx 400yd/360m of worsted weight yarn ❹ (A)

Blue Sky Alpacas Alpaca Silk (50% alpaca, 50% silk; 1.75oz/50g = 146yd/131m): 5 (6, 7) skeins, color chestnut #135—approx 730 (876, 1022)yd/657 (788, 920)m of sport weight yarn ❷ (B)

Knitting needles: 5.5mm (size 9 U.S.) straight and 16"/40.5cm circular needles *or size to obtain gauge*

Cable needle

Stitch markers

Tapestry needle

SKILL LEVEL
Experienced

SIZE
Women's S (M, L)

FINISHED MEASUREMENTS
Chest: 32 (38, 42)"/81 (97, 107)cm

Length: 26½ (27, 28)"/67 (69, 71)cm

Row 1 (WS): Sl 1, (with B) k2, (with A) p2, k2, p2, *(with B) k2, (with A) p2, k2, p2; rep from * to last st, k1.

Row 2: Sl 1, *(with A) k2, p2, k2, (with B) p2; rep from *, end (with A) k2, p2, k2, p2, k1.

Row 3: Rep row 1.

Row 4: Sl 1, *(with A) insert right needle from front to back between 6th and 7th sts on left needle and draw a loop through; slip this loop onto left needle and knit it tog with the 1st st on the same needle; k1, p2, k2, (with B) p2; rep from * to last st, k1.

Row 5: Rep row 1.

Row 6: Sl 1, *(with A/B) TW 3R, TW 3L, (with B) p2; rep from * to last st, (with B) k1.

Row 7: Sl 1, *(with B) k2, (with A) p2; rep from * to last st, (with B) k1.

Row 8: Sl 1, *(with A/B) TW 2R, (with B) p2, (with A/B) TW 2L, (with B) p2; rep from * to last st, (with B) k1.

Row 9 (Change to B completely): Sl 1, k4, *p2tog, k6; rep from * until last 5 sts, k2tog, k3.

instructions

BACK

With A, CO 90 (106, 122) sts.

Work in Smocking Rib pattern for 2 repeats (16 rows).

On the next WS row, with A and B, start Smocking-to-Rev St st Transition.

There will be 79 (93, 107) sts after row 9.

Continue in B only:

Row 1 (RS): Sl 1, p2, *k1, p6; rep from * to last 6 sts, k1, p4, k1.

Row 2: Sl 1, k4, *p1, k6; rep from * to last 4 sts, p1, k3.

Rep last 2 rows until piece measures 19 (19½, 20)"/48.5 (49.5, 51)cm.

ARMHOLE SHAPING:

BO 3 sts at beg of next 2 rows.

BO 2 sts at beg of following 4 rows.

BO 1 st at beg of the next 2 (2, 4) rows—63 (77, 89) sts.

Work even in established pattern until armhole measures 7½ (7½, 8)"/19 (19, 20.5)cm.

NECK SHAPING:

Work 19 (24, 28) sts, BO 25 (29, 33) sts, work remaining 19 (24, 28) sts.

Work both shoulders at the same time.

Next 2 (4, 4) rows: Work to last 2 sts, k2tog at neck edge; on opposite side, BO 1 st at neck edge, work to end—17 (20, 24) sts remaining for each shoulder.

BO.

my idea was to transition chunky smocking rib into a lightweight garment. The two fibers couldn't be too similar in weight, but not too different either. It had to be a perfect balance so that the body of the sweater still had substance.

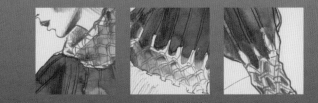

FRONT

Work same as for back until armholes measure 6 (6, 6½)"/15 (15, 16.5)cm.

NECK SHAPING:

Row 1: Work 22 (27, 31) sts, BO 19 (23, 27) sts, work remaining 22 (27, 31) sts.

Work both sides at once.

Next 5 (7, 7) rows: Work to last 2 sts, k2tog at neck edge; on opposite side, BO 1 st at neck edge, work to end—17 (20, 24) sts remaining for each shoulder.

Work even until piece measures same as for back rows, BO all sts.

SLEEVES (MAKE 2)

With A, CO 42 (50, 50) sts.

Work Smocking Rib pattern for 2 repeats (16 rows).

On the next WS row, with A and B, start Smocking-to-Rev St st Transition.

There will be 37 (44, 44) sts after row 9.

Change to B only.

Next row (RS): Inc 12 (29, 29) sts evenly across—59 (73, 73) sts.

Row 1 (WS): Sl 1, k9, p1, *k13, p1; rep from * to last 6 sts, k6.

Row 2 (RS): Sl 1, p5, *k1, p13; rep from * to last 11 sts, k1, p9, k1.

Rep last 2 rows until sleeves measure 19 (19½, 20)"/48.5 (49.5, 51) cm.

CAP SHAPING:

BO 3 sts at beg of next 2 rows.

BO 2 sts at beg of following 2 (4, 4) rows.

BO 1 st at beg of next 2 rows—47 (57, 57) sts.

Work even for 4 rows.

Rows 5, 6, 7, & 8: BO 1 st at beg of row—43 (53, 53) sts.

Repeat last 4 rows twice more—35 (45, 45) sts.

Next 2 (4, 4) rows: BO 1 st at beg of row—33 (41, 41) sts.

Next 4 rows: BO 2 sts at beg of row—25 (33, 33) sts.

Next 4 (6, 6) rows: BO 3 sts at beg of row—13 (15, 15) sts.

BO.

FINISHING

Block sweater to measurements before assembling.

Sew shoulder seams.

Using circular needle and A, pick up and knit 96 (104, 112) sts around neck opening, PM and join in a round.

Work in Smocking Rib pattern in the round as follows:

Rounds 1, 2, 3, 5, 6, & 7: *K2, p2; rep from * around.

Round 4: *Insert right needle between 6th and 7th st on left needle, wrap yarn around needle and pull up a loop, place loop on end of left needle (beside next st to be worked), k2tog (loop and 1st stitch), k1, p2, k2, p2; rep from * around.

Round 8: K2, p2, *insert right needle between 6th and 7th st on left needle and work as before, k2tog, k1, p2, k2, p2; rep from * to last 4 sts, insert needle after 1st 2 knit sts of next round (leave marker in place), wrap yarn and pull up a loop as before, k2tog, k1, p2.

Rep rounds 1-8 for pattern.

Work even until neck measures 10"/25cm. BO all sts in pattern. Attach sleeves, and sew side and sleeve seams. Weave in ends.

butterfly

CHAPTER 3

variations

enchanted by the editorial spreads in the April 1934 issue of *Harper's Bazaar*, I've created a chapter all about butterflies. Take a traditional butterfly pattern and let your imagination soar. Make the butterflies large or delicate, bead them up, or gather them together to shape the silhouette of each garment.

Very feminine in form, the draped shoulder cowl at the neck produces a dramatic outline that accentuates the shoulders.

cowl tank

SKILL LEVEL
Intermediate

SIZE
Women's S (M, L, 1X, 2X)

FINISHED MEASUREMENTS
Bust: 34 (37, 42, 46, 51)"/86.5 (94, 107, 117, 130)cm

Length: 20 (21, 22, 23, 24)"/51 (53.5, 56, 58.5, 61)cm

YOU WILL NEED

Classic Elite Wicked (100% cashmere; 1.75oz/50g = 165yd/149m): 6 (7, 8, 9, 10) skeins, color teal #10403—approx 990 (1155, 1320, 1485, 1650) yd/891 (1040, 1188, 1337, 1485)m of light worsted weight yarn **(3)**

Knitting needles: 4.5mm (size 7 U.S.) straight and 5mm (size 8 U.S.) 24"/61cm circular needle *or size to obtain gauge*

Stitch marker

Tapestry needle

GAUGE
18 sts and 26 rows = 4"/10cm in Butterfly stitch on smaller needles

Always take time to check your gauge.

SPECIAL ABBREVIATION
Gathering Stitch **(g-st):** On WS row, insert right needle under loose strands on RS of work, wrap yarn around needle, and pull this loop back under the loose strands, creating a st that gathers the loose strands.

PATTERN STITCH
Butterfly (multiple of 10 + 5):

Rows 1, 3, 5, 7, & 9 (RS): *Sl 5 wyif, k5; rep from * to last 5 sts, sl 5 wyif.

Rows 2, 4, 6, & 8: Purl.

Row 10 (WS): *P2, g-st, p1, pass g-st over st just worked, p9; rep from * to last 5 sts, p2, g-st, p1, pass g-st over st just worked, p2.

Rows 11, 13, 15, 17, & 19: *K5, sl 5 wyif; rep from * to last 5 sts, k5.

Rows 12, 14, 16, & 18: Purl.

Row 20: *P7, g-st, p1, pass g-st over st just worked, p2; rep from * to last 5 sts, p5.

Rep rows 1-20 for pattern.

FRONT AND BACK (MAKE 2)

Hem:

Using smaller needles, CO 75 (85, 95, 105, 115) sts.

Work in St st for ½"/1.5cm, ending with a RS row.

Next row (WS): Knit (create turning ridge for hem).

Work in St st for ½"/1.5cm more, ending with a WS row.

Next row (RS): Pick up a corresponding stitch of CO row and k2tog with every st on the needle.

BODY

Keeping first and last 5 sts of each row in St st and slipping 1st st of each row, work Butterfly pattern over center 65 (75, 85, 95, 105) sts for 3 (3, 3 ½, 3 ½, 3 ½)"/8 (8, 9, 9, 9)cm, ending with a WS row.

WAIST SHAPING:

Next (dec) row (RS): Sl 1, k2tog, k2, work in Butterfly pattern to last 5 sts, k2, ssk, k1—73 (83, 93, 103, 113) sts.

Then on the following 4th row, decrease again as follows:

Next (dec) row: Sl 1, k2tog, k1, work in Butterfly pattern to last 4 sts, k1, k2tog, k1—71 (81, 91, 101, 111) sts.

On following 4th row, decrease once more as follows:

Next (dec) row: Sl 1, k2tog, work in Butterfly pattern to last 3 sts, k2tog, k1—69 (79, 89, 99, 109) sts.

Keeping first and last 2 sts of each row in St st and slipping 1st st of each row, work Butterfly pattern as established for 1 (1, 1, 1½, 1½)"/2.5 (2.5, 2.5, 4, 4)cm, ending with a WS row.

Next (inc) row: Sl 1, M1, work as established to last st, M1, k1—71 (81, 91, 101, 111) sts.

Rep inc row every 6 rows twice more—75 (85, 95, 105, 115) sts.

Work even in pattern until piece measures 15 (15½, 16, 16½, 17)"/38 (39, 41, 42, 43)cm.

ARMHOLE SHAPING:

Row 1 (RS): BO 3 sts at beg of row, continue in established pattern across—72 (82, 92, 102, 112) sts.

Row 2: BO 3 sts at beg of row, work to last 2 sts, k2tog—68 (78, 88, 98, 108) sts.

Rows 3 & 4: BO 2 sts at beg of row, work to last 2 sts, k2tog—62 (72, 82, 92, 102) sts.

Rows 5 & 6: BO 1 st at beg of row, work to last 2 sts, k2tog—58 (68, 78, 88, 98) sts.

Rep rows 5 & 6, 0 (1, 1, 2, 2) times more—58 (64, 74, 80, 90) sts.

Next row: Work to last 2 sts, k2tog—57 (63, 73, 79, 89) sts.

Work even in pattern until piece measures 20 (21, 22, 23, 24)"/51 (53.5, 56, 58.5, 61)cm. BO.

SHOULDER PIECE

Using larger circular needles, CO 150 (161, 180, 195, 213) sts.

PM and join in a round, being careful not to twist the sts.

Hem:

Work in St st for ½"/1.5cm.

Next round (RS): Purl (create turning ridge for hem).

Work in St st for ½"/1.5cm more.

Next round (RS): Pick up a corresponding stitch of CO row and k2tog with every stitch on the needle.

MAIN SECTION:

Switch to smaller needles.

Work even in St st for 9"/23cm.

Then work in 1x1 rib for 2"/5cm.

BO in rib.

FINISHING

Sew the side seams.

Attach the rib section of the shoulder piece to the front and back body sections so that it folds over with the knit side showing. There should be 7 (7¼ , 7½, 7¾, 8)"/18 (18.5, 19, 19.5, 20) cm left for the arm openings.

GATHERING LOOP

Pick up and knit 13 sts at the center front right at the seam of front panel with shoulder top section.

Work in 1x1 rib for 5"/13cm. BO and attach BO edge to the WS of the same seam, gathering the shoulder piece inside the gathering loop.

Weave in ends.

This top was a double take on a butterfly, represented through both shape and stitch pattern. Before starting this piece, I swatched many yarns to see which would best resemble the grace of a butterfly. Cashmere seemed to be the best fit as it creates soft drapes.

In addition to
alluring texture, this
project features a
slimming design
element: waistline
gathers.

gathered cardigan

YOU WILL NEED

Alpaca Yarn Company Suri Elegance (100% Suri alpaca; 3.5oz/100g = 875yd/788m): 2 (2, 2) skeins, color Georgia Peach #3002—approx 1750yd/1575m of lace weight yarn 〔0〕

Knitting needles: 4mm (size 6 U.S.) 32"/81cm circular needle *or size to obtain gauge*

Crochet hook: 3.75mm (size F U.S.)

¼"(5mm) **ribbon,** 8yd (7m)

Stitch markers

Tapestry needle

SKILL LEVEL
Intermediate

SIZE
Women's S (M,L)

FINISHED MEASUREMENTS
Bust: 36 (40, 44)"/91 (102, 112)cm

Length: 28 (29½, 31)"/71 (75, 79)cm

GAUGE

22 sts/36 rows = 4"/10cm in Butterfly stitch

Always take time to check your gauge.

SPECIAL ABBREVIATIONS

Make one purl (M1p): Increase by picking up a bar between 2 sts, twisting and purling it.

Gathering Stitch (g-st): On WS row, insert right needle under loose strands on RS of work, wrap yarn around needle and pull this loop back under the loose strands, creating a st that gathers the loose strands.

PATTERN STITCHES

Butterfly (multiple of 10+5):

Rows 1, 3, 5, & 7 (RS): *Sl 5 wyif, k5; rep from * to last 5 sts, sl 5 wyif.

Rows 2, 4, & 6: Purl.

Row 8 (WS): *P2, g-st, p1, pass g-st over st just worked, p9; rep from * to last 5 sts, p2, g-st, p1, pass g-st over st just worked, p2.

Rows 9, 11, 13, & 15: *K5, sl 5 wyif; rep from * to last 5 sts, k5.

Rows 10, 12, & 14: Purl.

Row 16: *P7, g-st, p1, pass g-st over st just worked, p2; rep from * to last 5 sts, p5.

Rep rows 1-16 for pattern.

Picot Edge:

Rows 1, 3, & 5 (WS): Purl.

Rows 2 & 4: Knit.

Row 6: Sl 1, *k2tog, yo; rep from * to last st, k1.

Rows 7, 9, & 11: Purl.

Rows 8 &10: Knit.

Row 12: Pick up a corresponding stitch of CO row and knit tog with every st on the needle.

instructions

BODY

NOTE: Front and back are worked in one piece.

CO 197 (217, 237) sts.

Work Picot Edge pattern for the hem.

NOTE: Slip 1st st of every row throughout.

Next, starting with RS row, after slipping the first st, work Butterfly pattern over 195 (215, 235) sts, knit the last st.

Work even as established until piece measures 18 (19, 20)"/46 (48, 51)cm.

ARMHOLE SHAPING:

NOTE: PM after 51 (56, 61) sts from each side of the piece (these sts will become the left and right fronts).

Remaining 95 (105, 115) sts between markers will become the back of the sweater.

Continuing in Butterfly pattern as established, work to 3 sts before first marker, BO 6 sts, work to 3 sts before second marker, BO 6 sts, work remaining sts—48 (53, 58) sts for each front and 89 (99, 109) sts for the back.

NOTE: Work all 3 pieces at the same time in already established pattern, working each piece with a separate ball of yarn.

Rows 1 (WS) and 2: Work even in pattern to 2 sts before armhole, p2tog (k2tog on RS), on opposite side of armhole ssp (ssk on RS), work to 2 sts before second armhole, p2tog (k2tog on RS), on opposite side of armhole ssp (ssk on RS), work to end—46, 85, 46 [(51, 95, 51); (56, 105, 56)] sts.

Rep rows 1 & 2 twice more—42, 77, 42 [(47, 87, 47); (52, 97, 52)] sts.

Work even in pattern until armhole measures 1½"/4cm.

COLLAR SHAPING:

Row 1 (RS): Sl 1, k1, M1p, PM, work to end in established Butterfly pattern; work as established across back, work to last 2 sts, PM, M1p, k2—43 (48, 53) sts for fronts.

Row 2 (and every WS row): Knit all knit sts and purl all purl sts to marker, slip marker, work in pattern as established; work as established across back; work as established to marker, slip marker, knit all knit sts and purl all purl sts to end.

Row 3 (and every following RS row): Sl 1, [k1, M1p] to 2 sts after the marker, move marker, work to end in established Butterfly pattern; work as established across back; work in established Butterfly pattern to 1 st before marker, move marker, [M1p, k1] to last st, k1.

Rep rows 2 & 3 until there are 62 (67, 72) sts on each front. Work even as established until armhole measures 10 (10½, 11)"/25.5 (27, 28)cm, ending with a WS row.

SHOULDER SHAPING:

Next row (RS): Work in established rib pattern to marker, bind off rem 21 (24, 27) front sts for shoulder; bind off all sts across back, bind off first 21 (24, 27) sts for opposite front shoulder, work in established rib pattern to end.

Collar will be completed in 2 parts as follows:

Next row (WS): Work in established rib pattern, CO 35 (39, 43) sts for half of back collar; join second ball of yarn and CO 35 (39, 43) sts for other half of back collar, work in established rib pattern to end. Working both sides at once, continue in established rib pattern until back collar sts measure 2 (2½, 3)"/5 (6.5, 8)cm from CO row. BO.

When I began my initial sketches for this cardigan, I envisioned a very light, feminine, and delicate piece. In order to create soft gathers at the waist, I chose to work with lace weight alpaca, which created an airy fabric.

SLEEVES (MAKE 2)

CO 67 (77, 87) sts.

NOTE: Slip 1st st of every row throughout.

Next, starting with RS row, after slipping the first st, work Butterfly pattern over 65 (75, 85) sts, knit the last st.

Work even as established until piece measures 18 (18½, 19)"/46 (47, 48.5)cm.

CAP SHAPING:

Rows 1 (RS) & 2: BO 3 sts at beg of each row—61 (71, 81) sts.

Rows 3, 4, 5, & 6: BO 2 sts at beg of each row—53 (63, 73) sts.

Rows 7, 8, 9, & 10: BO 1 st at beg of each row—49 (59, 69) sts.

Work evenly in pattern until cap measures 5½"/14cm.

Dec 1 st at the beg & end of every RS row 5 (6, 7) times—39 (47, 55) sts.

BO 2 sts at beg of next 6 (8, 10) rows—27 (31, 35) sts.

BO 3 sts at beg of next 2 rows—21 (25, 29) sts.

BO 4 sts at beg of next 2 rows—13 (17, 21) sts.

BO.

FINISHING

Sew shoulder and side seams. Sew up and attach the sleeves. Attach the back collar, sewing center back seam and lower edge to back neck.

Using crochet hook, work 1 row of sc and 1 row of crab st on both front openings. Weave in ends.

Using ¼" (5mm) wide ribbon, weave 3 rows through the centers of butterflies at the waist area, make sure they stay flat, and then knot them together at the point they emerge from the center front. Cinch and tie as desired.

Beading emphasizes the butterfly pattern on this classy clutch that's perfect for an afternoon luncheon or an evening out.

beaded clutch

YOU WILL NEED

Blue Sky Alpacas Alpaca Silk (50% alpaca, 50% silk; 1.75oz/50g = 146yd/131m): 2 skeins, color oyster #115—approx 292yd/263m of sport weight yarn ②

Knitting needles: 3.75mm (size 5 U.S.) *or size to obtain gauge*

Crochet hook: 3.25mm (size D U.S.)

Stitch markers

Small seed beads, approx 320

Tapestry needle

14 x 14"/36 x 36cm piece of **flexible plastic** (optional)

15 x 15"/38 x 38cm piece of **lining fabric** (optional)

SKILL LEVEL
Intermediate

SIZE
One size

FINISHED MEASUREMENTS
14 x 4½"/ 36cm x 11.5, blocked and finished

GAUGE

30 sts and 36 rows = 4"/10cm in Butterfly stitch

Always take time to check your gauge.

SPECIAL ABBREVIATION

Gathering Stitch **(g-st):** On WS row, insert right needle under loose strands on RS of work, wrap yarn around needle and pull this loop back under the loose strands, creating a st that gathers the loose strands.

PATTERN STITCH

Butterfly (multiple of 14+7):

Rows 1, 3, 5, & 7 (RS): *Sl 7 wyif, k7; rep from * to last 7 sts, sl 7 wyif.

Rows 2, 4, & 6: Purl.

Row 8 (WS): *P3, g-st, p1, pass g-st over st just worked, p10; rep from * to last 7 sts, p3, g-st, p1, pass g-st over st just worked, p3.

Rows 9, 11, 13, & 15: *K7, sl 7 wyif; rep from * to last 7 sts, k7.

Rows 10, 12, & 14: Purl.

Row 16: *P10, g-st, p1, pass g-st over st just worked, p3; rep from * to last 7 sts, p7.

Rep rows 1-16 for pattern.

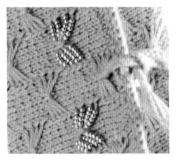

instructions

CLUTCH

Prestring 224 beads. CO 105 sts. Work first 8 rows of Butterfly pattern.

Continue to work Butterfly pattern, adding beads as follows:

Rows 9 & 11: Slide 10 beads on yarn held in front when slipping each group of 7 sts (beads rest in front of slipped sts).

Row 13: Slide 10 beads with each group of slipped sts.

Row 15: Slide 8 beads with each group of slipped sts.

NOTE: Loop the g-st on row 16 through the center of beads while creating a butterfly.

Continue working in Butterfly pattern for 5 more repeats (without beads), PM at each end of row (to mark bottom fold point). Work for 3 more pattern repeats ending with row 16.

Next 3 rows: Knit.

Row 4: Purl.

Rows: 5, 6, & 7: Work in St st.

BO.

BRAIDED TIES (MAKE 2)

Cut 6 lengths of yarn, each approx 20"/51cm long. Braid and fasten with an overhand knot, leaving approx 5"/13cm for fringe and one end.

FINISHING

Bend piece at markers and sew the side seams up to the garter ridge.

Lining (optional):

Cut flexible plastic to fit inside of bag. Trim lining fabric to 1"/2.5cm larger than plastic on all sides. Press ½"/1.5cm hem on fabric, place plastic behind fabric, allowing hem to cover edges. Insert in bag, whipstitch in place.

Attach and braid closure ties at center.

DESIGN TIP: This clutch looks much better when lined with flexible plastic behind the fabric to give it a better shape.

W hile experimenting with the butterfly pattern to see how far I could push it, I found myself stringing beads and creating three-dimensional beaded butterflies. Adding beads is a great way to create intriguing touches and exciting details.

tonal

CHAPTER 4

transitions

How do you make the standard stockinette stitch exciting again? With a different dimension. Smoothly changing fibers, textures, and colors give this basic stitch new life. The projects in this chapter illustrate how the stockinette stitch can create varying effects—from light to dark and lacy to heavy—as well as shift from one color to another for a look that is bold and dramatic.

kKnit in the round from transparent lace to a heavier, darker yarn, this skirt achieves a smooth tonal and textural transition, all in simple stockinette stitch.

tonal skirt

SKILL LEVEL
Intermediate

SIZE
Women's S (M,L)

FINISHED MEASUREMENTS
Hip: 33 (37, 41)"/84 (94, 104)cm

Length: 23 (23½, 24)"/58 (60, 61)cm

YOU WILL NEED

Artyarns Silk Mohair (60% super kid mohair, 40% silk; 0.88oz/25g = 312yd/281m): 1 skein, color cream #250—approx 312yd/281m of lace weight yarn (0) (A)

Artyarns Regal Silk (100% silk; 1.75oz/50g = 163yd/147m): (B) 1 skein, color light peach #223; (C) 1 skein, color dark peach #202; (D) 1 skein, color light gold #203; (E) 1 skein, color dark gold #201; (F) 1 skein, color brown #222—approx 815yd/734m of light worsted weight yarn (3)

Knitting needles: 6.5mm (size 10½ U.S.) 24"/61cm circular needle, 6mm (size 10 U.S.) 24"/61cm circular needle, 5.5mm (size 9 U.S.) 24"/61cm circular needle, 5mm (size 8 U.S.) 24"/61cm circular needle, 4.5mm (size 7 U.S.) 24"/61cm circular needle, 4mm (size 6 U.S.) 24"/61cm circular needle, and 3.75mm (size 5 U.S.) 24"/61cm circular needle *or size to obtain gauge*

Crochet hook: 2.75mm (size C U.S.)

Stitch markers in several colors

Bead or tiny button

Tapestry needle

GAUGE

30 sts and 32 rows = 4"/10cm in St st using heavier yarn and smallest needles

Always take time to check your gauge.

instructions

SKIRT

Using 1 strand of A and 6.5mm needles, CO 200 (230, 260) sts.

PM (center back) and join in a round, being careful not to twist the sts. Place 2nd marker 100 (115, 130) sts away from first marker (center front). Place 2 more markers at left and right side.

Work even in St st for 10 (12, 12) rounds.

Color Transition 1:

Round 1: Knit using 2 strands of A held double.

Rounds 2 & 3: Knit using 1 strand of A.

Rounds 4 & 5: Knit using 2 strands of A held double.

Round 6: Knit using 1 strand of A.

Next 6 rounds: Knit using 2 strands of A held double.

Color Transition 2:

Change to 6mm needles.

Round 1: Knit using B.

Rounds 2 & 3: Knit using 2 strands of A held double.

Rounds 4 & 5: Knit using B.

Round 6: Knit using 2 strands of A held double.

Next 16 (16, 18) rounds: Knit using B.

Color Transition 3:

Change to 5.5mm needles.

Round 1: Knit using C.

Rounds 2 & 3: Knit using B.

Rounds 4 & 5: Knit using C.

Round 6: Knit using B.

Next 20 rounds: Knit using C.

Color Transition 4:

Change to 5mm needles.

Round 1: Knit using D.

Rounds 2 & 3: Knit using C.

Rounds 4 & 5: Knit using D.

Round 6: Knit using C.

Continue as follows, using D.

Place different color markers 10 sts before and after front and back center markers (20 sts in between).

Round 1: Knit to the 1st front marker, slip marker, ssk, work to 2 sts before the 2nd front marker, k2tog, slip marker, knit to the 1st back marker, slip marker, ssk, work to 2 sts before the 2nd back marker, k2tog, slip marker, knit to end—196 (226, 256) sts.

Rounds 2, 3, 4, & 5: Knit to the 1st front marker, slip marker, ssk, M1, work to 2 sts before the 2nd front marker, M1, k2tog, slip marker, knit to the 1st back marker, slip marker, ssk, M1, work to 2 sts before the 2nd back marker, M1, k2tog, slip marker.

Place different color markers 8 sts before and after side left and side right markers (16 sts in between).

Round 6: Knit to the 1st front marker, slip marker, ssk, M1, work to 2 sts before the 2nd front marker, M1, k2tog, slip marker, knit to the 1st side left marker, slip marker, ssk, work to 2 sts before the 2nd side left marker, k2tog, slip marker, knit to the 1st back marker, slip marker, ssk, M1, work to 2 sts before the 2nd back marker, M1, k2tog, slip marker, knit to the 1st side right marker, slip marker, ssk, work to 2 sts before the 2nd side right marker, k2tog, slip marker—192 (222, 252) sts.

Rounds 7, 8, 9, & 10: Knit to the 1st front marker, *slip 1st marker, ssk, M1, work to 2 sts before the 2nd marker, M1, k2tog, slip marker; rep from * for side left, back, and side right markers.

Rep last 10 rounds once more without placing any new markers—184 (214, 244) sts.

Color Transition 5:

Change to 4.5mm needles and E.

Round 1: Place markers 8 sts before the first and after the last front and back markers.

Knit to the 1st front marker, *slip marker, ssk, work to the 2nd marker, slip marker, ssk, M1, work to 2 sts before the 3rd marker, M1, k2tog, slip marker, work to 2 sts before the 4th marker, k2tog, slip marker, work to the 1st side left marker, slip the 1st marker, ssk, M1, work to 2 sts before the 2nd marker, M1, k2tog, slip marker; rep from * for back and side right markers—180 (210, 240) sts.

Change to D.

Rounds 2 & 3: Knit to the 1st front marker, *slip the 1st marker, ssk, M1, work to the 2nd marker, slip marker, ssk, M1, work to 2 sts before the 3rd marker, M1, k2tog, slip marker, work to 2 sts before the 4th marker, M1, k2tog, slip marker, work to the 1st side left marker, slip marker, ssk, M1, work to 2 sts before the 2nd marker, M1, k2tog, slip marker; rep from * for back and side right markers.

Change to E.

Round 4: Place markers 8 sts before the first and after the last front and back markers.

Knit to the 1st front marker, *slip marker, ssk, work to the 2nd marker, slip marker, ssk, M1, work to the 3rd marker, slip marker, ssk, M1, work to 2 sts before the 4th marker, M1, k2tog, slip marker, work to 2 sts before the 5th marker, M1, k2tog, slip marker, work to 2 sts before the 6th marker, k2tog, slip marker, work to the 1st side left marker, slip marker, ssk, M1, work to 2 sts before the 2nd marker, M1, k2tog, slip marker; rep from * for back and side right markers—176 (206, 236) sts.

Rounds 5 (using E) and 6 (using D): Knit to the 1st front marker, *[slip marker, ssk, M1] three times, [work to 2 sts before the next marker, M1, k2tog, slip marker] three times, work to the 1st side left marker, slip marker, ssk, M1, work to 2 sts before the 2nd marker, M1, k2tog, slip marker; rep from * for back and side right markers.

Continue as follows, using E.

Place markers 8 sts before the first and after the last front and back markers.

Round 1: Knit to the 1st front marker, *slip marker, ssk, [work to the next marker, slip marker, ssk, M1] three times, [work to 2 sts before the next marker, M1, k2tog, slip marker] three times, work to 2 sts before the next marker, k2tog, slip marker, work to the 1st side left marker, slip marker, ssk, M1, work to 2 sts before the 2nd marker, M1, k2tog, slip marker; rep from * for back and side right markers—172 (202, 232) sts.

Rounds 2 and 3: Knit to the 1st front marker, *[slip marker, ssk, M1] four times, [work to 2 sts before the next marker, M1, k2tog, slip marker] four times, work to the 1st side left marker, slip marker, ssk, M1, work to 2 sts before the 2nd marker, M1, k2tog, slip marker; rep from * for back and side right markers.

Round 4: *[Work to the next marker, slip marker, ssk, M1] three times, knit to the next marker, slip marker, ssk, work to 2 sts before the next marker, k2tog, slip marker, [work to 2 sts before the next marker, M1, k2tog, slip marker] three times, work to the 1st side left marker, slip marker, ssk, work to 2 sts before the 2nd marker, k2tog, slip marker; rep from * for back and side right markers—164 (194, 224) sts.

Change to 4mm needles.

Rounds 5 & 6: Rep rounds 2 & 3.

Round 7: *[Work to the next marker, slip marker, ssk, M1] two times, knit to the next marker, slip marker, ssk, work to the next marker, slip marker, ssk, M1, work to 2 sts before the next marker, M1, k2tog, slip marker, work to 2 sts before the next marker, k2tog, slip marker, [work to 2 sts before the next marker, M1, k2tog, slip marker] twice, work to the 1st side left marker, slip marker, ssk, work to 2 sts before the 2nd marker, k2tog, slip marker; rep from * for back and side right markers—160 (190, 220) sts.

Round 8: *[Work to the next marker, slip marker, ssk, M1] once, knit to the next marker, slip marker, ssk, [work to the next marker, slip marker, ssk, M1] twice, [work to 2 sts before the next marker, M1, k2tog, slip marker] twice, work to 2 sts before the next marker, k2tog, slip marker, [work to 2 sts before the next marker, M1, k2tog, slip marker] once, work to the 1st side left marker, slip marker, ssk,

work to 2 sts before the 2nd marker, k2tog, slip marker; rep from *
for back and side right markers—156 (186, 216) sts.

Round 9: *Knit to the next marker, slip marker, ssk, [work to the next
marker, slip marker, ssk, M1] three times, [work to 2 sts before the
next marker, M1, k2tog, slip marker] three times, work to 2 sts before
the next marker, k2tog, slip marker, work to the 1st side left marker,
slip the marker, ssk, work to 2 sts before the 2nd marker, k2tog, slip
marker; rep from * for back and side right markers—152 (182, 212) sts.

Rep rounds 7, 8, & 9 once more—140 (170, 200) sts.

Rep round 2 for 10 more rounds.

Color Transition 6:

Change to 3.75mm needles and 1x1 rib.

Round 1: Work using F.

Rounds 2 & 3: Work using E.

Rounds 4 & 5: Work using F.

Round 6: Work using E.

Round 7: Work using F.

Continue in F.

On round 8, stop working in round and split in the center back, continuing in 1x1 rib.

Work back and forth in 1x1 rib for 10 more rows. BO loosely in pattern.

FINISHING

With crochet hook and F, join yarn to right side of back opening.
Work chain long enough to fit button, sl st in place to form loop,
and fasten off. Sew button opposite loop. Weave in ends.

Form meets function here: through a
seamless pattern we create a continuous shape as well as a perfectly
functional object. I wanted the piece—
knit on a circular needle—to transition
from light and airy to something more
substantial, but very slowly and gradually. I started with one strand of thin, fine
lace weight mohair, began doubling it,
started combining different fibers, then
changed up the needle sizes, and finished by utilizing the decreases.

tube scarf

Worked in the round, this dramatic scarf features two transitions: light colors to dark and lightweight yarn to heavy.

YOU WILL NEED

Artyarns Silk Mohair (60% super kid mohair, 40% silk; 0.88oz/25g = 312yd/281m): 1 skein, color cream #250—approx 312yd/281m of lace weight yarn (0) (A)

Artyarns Regal Silk (100% silk; 1.75oz/50g = 163yd/147m): (B) 1 skein, color light peach #223; (C) 1 skein, color dark peach #202; (D) 1 skein, color light gold #203; (E) 1 skein, color dark gold #201; (F) 1 skein, color red #218—approx 815yd/734m of light worsted weight yarn (3)

Knitting needles: 6mm (size 10 U.S.) 16"/40.5cm circular needle, 4.5mm (size 7 U.S.) 16"/40.5cm circular needle and 3.75mm (size 5 U.S.) 12"/30.5cm circular needle *or size to obtain gauge*

Stitch markers

Tapestry needle

SKILL LEVEL
Intermediate

SIZE
One size

FINISHED MEASUREMENTS
7 x 104"/18 x 264cm at widest point

GAUGE

28 sts and 30 rows = 4"/10cm in St st using heavier yarn and smallest needles

Always take time to check your gauge.

instructions

SCARF

Using A and 6mm needles, CO 66 sts.

PM and join in a round, being careful not to twist the sts.

Work evenly in St st for 10 rounds.

Color Transition 1:

Round 1: Knit using B.

Rounds 2 & 3: Knit using A.

Rounds 4 & 5: Knit using B.

Round 6: Knit using A.

Change to 4.5mm needles.

Next 22 rounds: Knit using B.

Color Transition 2:

Round 1: Knit using C.

Rounds 2 & 3: Knit using B.

Rounds 4 & 5: Knit using C.

Round 6: Knit using B.

Change to 3.75mm needles.

Next 33 rounds: Knit using C.

Color Transition 3:

Round 1: Knit using D.

Rounds 2 & 3: Knit using C.

Rounds 4 & 5: Knit using D.

Round 6: Knit using C.

Continue as follows using D.

Next (dec) round: Sl 1, k2tog, psso, work 30 sts, PM, sl 1, k2tog, psso, work to end of round—62 sts.

Work even for 5 rounds, stopping 1 st before the first marker.

Next (dec) round: Slip marker, sl 1, k2tog, psso, replace marker, work to 1 st before the second marker, slip marker, sl 1, k2tog, psso, replace marker, work to end of round—58 sts.

Rep last 6 rounds 5 more times—38 sts.

Next 7 rounds: Knit using D.

Color Transition 4:

Round 1: Knit using E.

Rounds 2 & 3: Knit using D.

Rounds 4 & 5: Knit using E.

Round 6: Knit using D.

Next 68 rounds: Knit using E.

Color Transition 5:

Round 1: Knit using F.

Rounds 2 & 3: Knit using E.

Rounds 4 & 5: Knit using F.

Round 6: Knit using E.

Work even in F for 20"/51cm.

Color Transition 6:

Round 1: Knit using E.

Rounds 2 & 3: Knit using F.

Rounds 4 & 5: Knit using E.

Round 6: Knit using F.

Next 68 rounds: Knit using E.

Color Transition 7:

Round 1: Knit using D.

Rounds 2 & 3: Knit using E.

Rounds 4 & 5: Knit using D.

Round 6: Knit using E.

Continue as follows using D.

Next (inc) round: M1, PM, k1, PM, M1, work 30 sts, M1, PM, k1, PM, M1, work to end of round—42 sts.

Work evenly for 5 rounds, stopping at the 1st inc marker.

Next (inc) round: M1, slip marker, k1, slip marker, M1, work to the second set of inc markers, M1, slip marker, k1, slip marker, M1, work to end of round—46 sts.

Work evenly for 5 rounds stopping at the 1st increase marker.

Rep last 6 rounds 5 more times—66 sts.

Next 7 rounds: Knit using D.

Color Transition 8:

Round 1: Knit using C.

Rounds 2 & 3: Knit using D.

Rounds 4 & 5: Knit using C.

Round 6: Knit using D.

Next 33 rounds: Knit using C.

Change to 4.5mm needles.

Color Transition 9:

Round 1: Knit using B.

Rounds 2 & 3: Knit using C.

Rounds 4 & 5: Knit using B.

Round 6: Knit using C.

Next 22 rounds: Knit using B.

Change to 6mm needles.

Color Transition 10:

Round 1: Knit using A.

Rounds 2 & 3: Knit using B.

Rounds 4 & 5: Knit using A.

Round 6: Knit using B.

Next 10 rounds: Knit using A.

BO loosely.

FINISHING

Weave in ends.

This scarf incorporates everything I discovered about the tonal knitting technique in stockinette stitch. The piece transitions between fibers and colors, and is shaped along the way so that it flares on each side. The most exciting part was the idea of working it on a circular needle—which made the scarf tubular and seamless.

From the front, this tank has a simple, appealing profile, created with a standard rib stitch. The back provides the surprise: a flirty lace insert.

lacy halter

SKILL LEVEL
Experienced

SIZE
Women's S/M (L/XL)

FINISHED MEASUREMENTS
Bust: 36 (42)"/91 (107)cm

Length: 25"/64cm, excluding straps

YOU WILL NEED

Lorna's Laces Helen's Lace (50% silk, 50% wool; 4oz/114g = 1250yd/1125m): 1 skein, color jeans #46—approx 1250yd/1125m of lace weight yarn 🔟 (A)

Lorna's Laces Shepherd Sock (80% superwash wool, 20% nylon; 1.75oz/50g = 215yd/194m): 1 skein, color pioneer #16—approx 215yd/194m of fingering weight yarn 🔟 (B)

Lorna's Laces Lion and Lamb (50% silk, 50% wool; 3.5oz/100g = 205yd/185m): 2 skeins, color navy #24—approx 410yd/369m of worsted weight yarn 🔟 (C)

Knitting needles: 6mm (size 10 U.S.) 24"/61cm circular needle and double-pointed needles *or size to obtain gauge*

Stitch holder

Stitch markers

Tapestry needle

20 sts and 22 rows = 4"/10cm in heaviest yarn in 1x1 rib, slightly stretched

Always take time to check your gauge.

instructions

TANK

Using A, CO 150 (180) sts.

PM and join in round, being careful not to twist the sts.

Work even in St st for 6 rounds.

Round 7: *P1, k2tog, p1, k26; rep from * around—145 (174) sts.

Rounds 8, 9, 10, & 11: *P1, k1, p1, k26; rep from * around.

Rounds 12, 13, 14, & 15: *P1, (k1, p1) twice, k22, p1, k1; rep from * around.

Rounds 16, 17, 18, & 19: *P1, (k1, p1) three times, k18, (p1, k1) twice; rep from * around.

Rounds 20, 21, 22, & 23: *P1, (k1, p1) four times, k14, (p1, k1) three times; rep from * around.

Rounds 24 & 26 (with B): *P1, (k1, p1) five times, k10, (p1, k1) four times; rep from * around.

Rounds 25 & 27 (with A): *P1, (k1, p1) five times, k10, (p1, k1) four times; rep from * around.

Stop using color A and change to color B completely.

Rounds 28, 29, 30, & 31: *P1, (k1, p1) six times, k6, (p1, k1) five times; rep from * around.

Rounds 32, 33, 34, & 35: *P1, (k1, p1) seven times, k2tog, (p1, k1) six times; rep from * around—140 (168) sts.

Rounds 36, 38, & 40 (with C): *P1, k1; rep from * around.

Rounds 37 & 39 (with B): *P1, k1; rep from * around.

Round 41: Work 27 sts in C, PM, k1 in A, PM, work in 1x1 rib to end of round. Remove beginning of the round marker.

Next round: Work in established rib pattern in C to 1 st before the 1st marker, *move markers apart by 1 st (3 sts between markers), knit sts between markers in A, wrap & turn once you reach the 2nd marker, purl sts between markers in A, work in 1x1 rib in C to 1 st before the marker, move markers apart by 1 st (5 sts between markers), purl sts between markers in A, wrap & turn, knit sts between markers in A, work in 1x1 rib in C to the marker again; rep from * until there are 65 sts in A between markers.

Work to the next marker, *(do not move markers apart by 1 st) M1, work sts in between the markers in A, M1, wrap & turn, work sts between markers in A, work in 1x1 rib in C to the marker again; rep from * until there are 91 (93) sts in A between markers.

Work to the next marker, *purl sts between markers in B, wrap & turn, purl sts between markers in B, work in 1x1 rib in C to the marker again; rep from * once more.

BO all sts between the markers in B.

Work evenly in established rib pattern in C for 7"/18cm. Work the last row very loosely and put live sts on the holder.

FINISHING

Using C and double-pointed needles, CO 3 sts and knit in I-cord for 44"/112cm.

Slide cord through all live sts for the front. Weave it through the top edge of the back lace panel. Tie about 4"/10cm on each side of cord into a knot.

Secure the last live st. Weave in ends.

This tank is the most experimental piece in the Tonal chapter since it's based on rib instead of stockinette stitch, has a tonal lace insert, and is knit in the round. Despite the complexity of the piece, it was still possible to create a sensual, body-hugging garment.

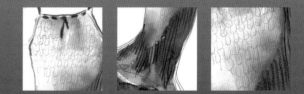

herringbone

CHAPTER 5

evolution

Herringbone is another classic stitch pattern that needs spicing up. Taking a cue from geometric patterns found in nature, I incorporated different colors or textural elements, like leather, into the existing stitch pattern.

A play with textures creates an optical trick that disguises the leather integrated within the pattern.

herringbone purse

Artyarns Silk Rhapsody (100% silk core, wrapped in 70% mohair/30% silk; 3.5oz/100g = 260yd/234m): 5 skeins, color rose natural #137—approx 1300yd/1170m of worsted weight yarn 〔4〕 (A)

⅛" (3mm) **leather lacing** (100% leather; 100yd/90m): 4 balls, color peach #12—approx 400yd/360m (B)

Knitting needles: 6mm (size 10 U.S.) straight and double-pointed needles *or size to obtain gauge*

Crochet hook: 3.75mm (size F U.S.)

Cable needle

Stitch markers

Stitch holders

18 x 35"/46 x 89cm **piece of lining fabric**

Sewing needle and thread

Pearl beads (optional)

Tapestry needle

SKILL LEVEL
Experienced

SIZE
One size

FINISHED MEASUREMENTS
13 x 17"/33 x 43cm, excluding handles, across top

GAUGE

32 sts and 24 rows = 4"/10cm in Herringbone stitch

Always take time to check your gauge.

SPECIAL ABBREVIATIONS

6-st RC: Sl 3 sts to cn and hold in back of work, k3, k3 from cn.

6-st LC: Sl 3 sts to cn and hold in front of work, k3, k3 from cn.

5-st RC: Sl 2 sts to cn and hold in back of work, k3, k2 from cn.

5-st LC: Sl 3 sts to cn and hold in front of work, k2, k3 from cn.

4-st RC: Sl 2 sts to cn and hold in back of work, k2, k2 from cn.

4-st LC: Sl 2 sts to cn and hold in front of work, k2, k2 from cn.

PATTERN STITCH

Herringbone (multiple of 36 + 28 sts):

Row 1 (RS): K2, 6-st RC, [k3, 6-st RC] 2 times, *k3, 6-st LC, [k3, 6-st RC] 3 times; rep from *, end k2.

Row 2 and all WS rows: Purl.

Row 3: K8, 6-st RC, k3, 6-st RC, *[6-st LC, k3] twice, k3, 6-st RC, k3, 6-st RC; rep from *, end k5.

Row 5: K5, [6-st RC, k3] twice, *k3, 6-st LC, k3, 6-st LC, [6-st RC, k3] twice; rep from *, end k5.

Row 6: Purl.

Rep rows 1-6 for pattern.

instructions

FRONT AND BACK (MAKE 2)

Using 2 strands of A held double, CO 66 sts.

Row 1 (and every WS row): Purl.

Row 2: Sl 1, PM, work in Herringbone pattern (row 1 of pattern st) to last stitch, PM, k1—pattern on center 64 sts.

Row 4: Work in pattern, CO 3 sts at the end of the row.

Row 5: Sl 1, purl to end, CO 3 sts—72 sts.

Row 6: Knit to first marker, work in Herringbone pattern as established over 64 sts to second marker, knit remaining sts.

Row 7: Purl.

Rows 8 and 9: Rep rows 4 and 5—78 sts.

Rows 10 and 11: Rep rows 6 and 7.

Row 12 (pat row 5): Knit to 4 sts before first marker, move marker to this point, continue in pattern as follows: k3, 6-st LC, [6-st RC, k3] twice, *k3, 6-st LC, k3, 6-st LC, [6-st RC, k3] twice; rep from * (second time through only), end k3, 6-st LC, move marker after LC, k2, CO 4–82 sts.

Row 13: Sl 1, purl to end, move marker, CO 4 sts–86 sts.

Row 14 (pat row 1): Sl 1, move marker, work row 1 of Herringbone pattern from *, end k3, 6-st LC, k3, move marker, k1.

Rows 15 & 17: Purl.

Row 16 (pat row 3): Sl 1, k3, [6-st LC, k3] once, k3, 6-st RC, k3, 6-st RC, *[6-st LC, k3] twice, k3, 6-st RC, k3, 6-st RC; rep from *, end [6-st LC, k3] twice, k1.

Row 18 (pat row 5): Sl 1, k8, 6-st LC, [6-st RC, k3] twice, *k3, 6-st LC, k3, 6-st LC, [6-st RC, k3] twice; rep from * (second time through only), end k3, 6-st LC, move marker after LC, k8, move marker, CO 4–90 sts.

Row 19: Rep row 13–94 sts.

Row 20 (pat row 1): Sl 1, k3, work row 1 of Herringbone pattern from *, end k3, 6-st LC, k8, move marker, k1, CO 4–98 sts.

Row 21: Rep row 13–102 sts.

Rep row 2, working Herringbone pattern over center 100 sts.

Rep rows 3-21 once more—138 sts.

Work even in pattern, moving markers to 1 st from each end (slipping 1st st of each row) and working in pattern over center 136 sts until piece measures 5"/13cm from beg, ending with row 6 of pattern.

Begin first set of decreases on the next row 1 of the pattern repeat:

Row 1: *Work in pattern to last 2 sts of cable, k2tog, (that is, [work in pattern to last 2 sts of cable, k2tog] 3 times; rep from * to last st, k1–124 sts.

Rows 2-6: Work in pattern, working all cables as either 5-st LC or 5-st RC.

Begin second set of decreases on the next row 1 of the pattern repeat:

Row 1: Rep row 1 of first set of decreases—110 sts.

Rows 2-6: Work in pattern, working all cables as either 4-st LC or 4-st RC.

Work even in pattern until piece measures 13"/33cm from beg, ending with row 6 of pattern.

Row 1: Work as established, joining B at each 4-st RC, and working those cables as follows: sl 2 sts (in A) to cn and hold to back, join B and knit 2 sts in B, knit 2 sts from cn (in A).

Continue in pattern, using B as established, until piece measures 17"/43cm, ending with row 5. Do not cut B, place sts worked in B on holders.

Next row (WS): Using A, knit (create turning ridge for hem).

Work in St st for 1"/2.5cm. BO.

O ften my inspirational source is a traditional stitch pattern that I twist and turn and develop into something new or something that helps to create an exciting form or detail—this is what happened with the Herringbone Purse. While experimenting with different fibers, I discovered how perfectly leather lace worked as a part of the herringbone. Revisiting the concept of form and function, the leather inserts became a handle.

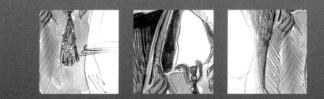

FINISHING

There are 4 leather lace sections, each having 3 strips on each side.

Using double-pointed needles, work each leather lace strip of the side sections (leave the two middle sections unworked for now) separately in I-cord for 3"/8cm. On first row, work kfb, k1—3 sts.

Then put each strip on a separate double-pointed needle and join in a round—9 sts. Work 1 round even.
Next round: [K1, k2tog] 3 times—6 sts.

Leave one side section as it is on a holder and continue working 6 sts of the other side section in the round until it measures 14"/36cm.

Graft the sts of the cord to the 6 sts of the other side section from the holder using Kitchener stitch.

Wrap the tail around the joins on both sides and tuck in tightly.

CLOSURE LOOP:

Divide each strip of each one of the center panels onto 3 double-pointed needles, work 2 rounds even—6 sts.

Next round: [K2tog] 3 times—3 sts.

Leave one center section as it is on a holder and continue working 3 sts of the other side section in the round until it measures 3"/8cm.

Graft the sts of the cord to the 3 sts of the other side section from the holder using Kitchener stitch.

Wrap the tail around the joins on both sides and tuck in tightly.

Closure tassel:

K2tog the sts of each remaining strip of both center panels.

Add extra strings of B and using crochet hook, crochet them tog in a chain for 3"/8cm.

Tie all 6 crochet chains tog and trim with 7"/18cm tassel, accented with pearl beads if desired.

Leave 5½"/14cm slit openings at the top on both sides, and sew the rest of the side seams together.

Cut lining to fit, allowing ½"/1cm for seam allowances. Sew side seams of lining, fold down ½"/1cm from top edge, and press. Insert lining in bag. Fold knitting hems over lining and neatly whipstitch in place.

cashmere muffler

The stylish neckwarmer holds its shape at the neck—keeping you nice and warm—and then drapes dramatically over the shoulders.

SIZE
One size

FINISHED MEASUREMENTS
Bottom circumference: 38"/97cm

Top circumference: 24"/61cm

Length: 20"/51cm

YOU WILL NEED

Artyarns Cashmere 5 (100% cashmere; 1.75oz/50g = 102yd/92m): 4 skeins, color rose natural #137—approx 408yd/367m of worsted weight yarn ⑷

Knitting needles: 6mm (size 10 U.S.) *or size to obtain gauge*

Cable needle

Stitch marker

Tapestry needle

GAUGE

23 sts and 24 rows = 4"/10cm in Herringbone stitch

Always take time to check your gauge.

SPECIAL ABBREVIATIONS

6-st RC: Sl 3 sts to cn and hold in back of work, k3, k3 from cn.

6-st LC: Sl 3 sts to cn and hold in front of work, k3, k3 from cn.

5-st RC: Sl 2 sts to cn and hold in back of work, k3, k2 from cn.

5-st LC: Sl 3 sts to cn and hold in front of work, k2, k3 from cn.

4-st RC: Sl 2 sts to cn and hold in back of work, k2, k2 from cn.

4-st LC: Sl 2 sts to cn and hold in front of work, k2, k2 from cn.

PATTERN STITCH

Herringbone in Round (multiple of 36 sts):

Round 1(RS): *K3, 6-st LC, [k3, 6-st RC] 3 times; rep from * around.

NOTE: Move the marker back 3 sts after working every round 1 to adjust sts in preparation for round 3, to 3 sts before end of round.

Round 2 and all even-numbered rounds: Knit.

Round 3: *[6-st LC, k3] twice, k3, 6-st RC, k3, 6-st RC; rep from * around.

Round 5: *K3, 6-st LC, k3, 6-st LC, [6-st RC, k3] twice; rep from * around.

NOTE: Move the marker forward 3 sts after working round 5 to return marker to its original location in preparation for round 1.

Round 6: Knit.

Rep rounds 1–6 for pattern.

instructions

NECKWARMER

CO 216 sts. PM and join in a round, being careful not to twist the sts.

Work in Herringbone in Round pattern for 5 pattern repeats (30 rounds), making sure to move the marker as indicated above.

Begin first set of decreases on the next round 1 of the pattern repeat:

Round 1: *Work in pattern to last 2 sts of cable, k2tog, (that is, [work in pattern to last 2 sts of cable, k2tog] 3 times); rep from * around—192 sts.

Rounds 2–6: Work in pattern, working all cables as either 5-st LC or 5-st RC.

Begin second set of decreases on the next round 1 of the pattern repeat:

Round 1: Rep round 1 of first set of decreases—168 sts.

Rounds 2–6: Work in pattern, working all cables as either 4-st LC or 4-st RC.

Begin third set of decreases on the next round 1 of the pattern repeat:

Round 1: *K1, k2tog, 4-st LC, [k1, k2tog, 4-st RC] 3 times; rep from * around—144 sts.

Rounds 2–6: Work in pattern, working k2 instead of k3.

Work even in pattern until piece measures 20"/51cm. BO loosely.

FINISHING

Weave in ends.

Here I was experimenting with shaping and decreasing within the pattern while simultaneously knitting in a round—quite a different idea than working the pattern on a straight needle.

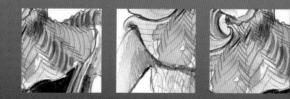

cable

magic

Intrigued by the way ice forms along a frosted window,
I reinvented a simple cable by shaping within the cables and creating lace
inserts. The designs on the following pages illustrate this technique, which
works across a wide array of projects from hats to skirts to blankets.
You'll have the most fun you've ever had with cables.

This seamless cable skirt achieves its sensuous lines through shaping within the pattern, including decreases and changes in needle size.

cable skirt

SKILL LEVEL
Intermediate

SIZE
Women's S (M, L,XL)

FINISHED MEASUREMENTS
Waist: 26 (28, 30, 32)"/66 (71, 76, 81)cm

Length: 21 (22, 23, 24½)"/53.5 (56, 58, 62)cm

YOU WILL NEED

Blue Sky Alpacas Royal (100% alpaca; 3.5oz/100g = 288yd/259m): 4 (4, 5, 5) skeins, color patina #707—approx 1152 (1152, 1440, 1440)yd/1037 (1037, 1296, 1296)m of sport weight yarn ②

Knitting needles: 6mm (size 10 U.S.) 32"/81.5cm circular needle, 5mm (size 8 U.S.) 24"/61cm circular needle, 4.5mm (size 7 U.S.) 24"/61cm circular needle *or size to obtain gauge*

Crochet hook: 3.75mm (size F U.S.)

Cable needle

Small button

Tapestry needle

GAUGE

18 sts and 28 rows = 4"/10cm over [C4F, k3] repeat using smallest needles and 2 strands of yarn held double

Always take time to check your gauge.

SPECIAL ABBREVIATION

C10F: Sl 5 sts to cn and hold in front of work, k5, k5 from cn.

C8F: Sl 4 sts to cn and hold in front of work, k4, k4 from cn.

C6F: Sl 3 sts to cn and hold in front of work, k3, k3 sts from cn.

C4F: Sl 2 sts to cn and hold in front of work, k2, k2 sts from cn.

instructions

SKIRT

Using 6mm and 2 strands of yarn held double, CO 221 (234, 247, 260) sts.

PM and join in a round, being careful not to twist the sts.

Round 1: Knit.

Round 2: Purl.

Rep last 2 rounds once more.

Establish cable repeat:

Rounds 1-4: *K10, p3; rep from * around.

Round 5: *C10F, p3; rep from * around.

Rounds 6-14: *K10, p3; rep from * around.

Round 15: *C10F, p3; rep from * around.

Rep rounds 6–15 once more.

Next cable section:

Round 1 (dec): *K3, k2tog, k2tog, k3, p3; rep from * around—187 (198, 209, 220) sts.

Rounds 2-9: *K8, p3; rep from * around.

Round 10: *C8F, p3; rep from * around.

Rep rounds 2–10, 1 (1, 1, 2) times more.

Change to 5mm needles.

Next cable section:

Rounds 1–7: *K8, p3; rep from * around.

Round 8: *C8F, p3; rep from * around.

Rep rounds 1-8 once more.

Next round (dec): *K2, k2tog, k2tog, k2, p3; rep from * around—153 (162, 171, 180) sts.

Next cable section:

Rounds 1–6: *K6, p3; rep from * around.

Round 7: *C6F, p3; rep from * around.

Rep rounds 1-7, 3 (4, 5, 5) times more.

Change to 4.5mm needles.

Next cable section:

Rounds 1–5: *K6, p3; rep from * around.

Round 6: *C6F, p3; rep from * around.

Next round (dec): *K1, k2tog, k2tog, k1, p3; rep from * around—119 (126, 133, 140) sts.

Last cable section:

Rounds 1–4: *K4, p3; rep from * around.

Round 5: *C4F, p3; rep from * around.

Rep rounds 1-5 four times more.

WAISTBAND:

Next row: K2, stop working in a round, turn (for back opening keyhole).

Row 1 (WS) and every following WS row: Knit all knit sts and purl all purl sts.

Row 2 (RS): Rep row 1.

Row 4: K2, p3, *(C4F, p3); rep from * to last 2 sts, k2.

Knit 3 more rows. BO.

FINISHING

On left side of keyhole opening and using crochet hook and single strand of yarn, join yarn with a sl st and crochet a chain loop large enough for button. Join in place with a sl st, and fasten off. Weave in ends. Sew button opposite buttonhole.

The technique of decreasing within the cables is really the best way to create a shape you want. Cables can be very forgiving when you decrease them and provide your finished garment a seamless look.

Decreasing gradually within the cables, this hat has a loose, yet cozy fit—complete with fun bobbles.

bobble hat

SKILL LEVEL
Experienced

SIZE
Women's

FINISHED MEASUREMENTS
**Head circumference:
21"/53.5cm**

YOU WILL NEED

Artyarns Silk Rhapsody (100% silk core, wrapped in 70% mohair/30% silk; 3.5oz/100g = 260yd/234m): 1 skein, color gray/blue #149—approx 260yd/234m of worsted weight yarn **4**

Knitting needles: 5.5mm (size 9 U.S.) 16"/40.5cm circular needle and double-pointed needles *or size to obtain gauge*

Cable needle

Stitch marker

Tapestry needle

GAUGE

18 sts and 32 rows = 4"/10cm in St st

Always take time to check your gauge.

SPECIAL ABBREVIATIONS

M1B: Increase by picking up a bar between 2 sts, twisting it and putting it onto the left needle, then knit into the front and back of this stitch twice (4 new sts made), turn; sl 1, p3, turn; sl 2, k3, turn; sl 1, p3, turn; sl 1, k2tog, k1, turn; p3tog, turn and slip this stitch onto the right needle (bobble made).

MB: Knit into the front and back of the next stitch twice, turn; sl 1, p3, turn; sl 2, k3, turn; sl 1, p3, turn; sl 1, k2tog, k1, turn; p3tog, turn and slip this stitch onto the right needle (bobble made).

C6F: Sl 3 sts to cn and hold in front of work, k3, k3 sts from cn.

C6-5F: Sl 3 sts to cn and hold in front of work, k2tog, k1, k3 from cn.

C5-4F: Sl 2 sts to cn and hold in front of work, k2tog, k1, k2 from cn.

C4F: Sl 2 sts to cn and hold in front of work, k2, k2 sts from cn.

C3-2F: Sl 2 sts to cn and hold in front of work, k2tog, k1 from cn.

C4-3F: Sl 2 sts to cn and hold in front of work, k2tog, k2 from cn.

instructions

HAT

CO 104 sts.

PM and join in round, being careful not to twist the sts.

Round 1: *K2 , p2; rep from * to end of round.

Rep last round until piece measures 1½"/4cm.

Begin cable pattern:

Round 1: *C6F, p1, M1B, p1; rep from * to end of round.

Rounds 2, 3, 4, 5, 6, & 7: Knit all knit sts and purl all purl sts.

Round 8: *C6F, p3; rep from * to end of round.

Rep rounds 2–7 once more.

Work round 1 again.

Rep rounds 2–7 once more.

Then dec within a cable as follows: *C6-5F, p3; rep from * to end of round—91 sts.

Rep rounds 2–6.

Then dec within a cable as follows: *C5-4F, p1, MB, p1; rep from * to end of round—78 sts.

Rep rounds 2-5.

Then dec sts between the cables as follows: *C4F, p3tog; rep from * to end of round—52 sts.

Rep rounds 2–4.

Then dec within a cable as follows: *C4-3F, MB; rep from * to end of round—39 sts.

Rep rounds 2-3.

Then dec within a cable as follows: *C3-2F, p1; rep from * to end of round—26 sts.

Next round: Rep round 2.

Next (dec) round: *K2tog, p1; rep from * to end of round—13 sts.

Next (dec) round: *K2tog; rep from * to last st, k1—7 sts.

Cut a long tail of yarn, slip through remaining sts and secure. Fasten off.

FINISHING

Weave in ends.

Here's another example of putting cable decreases to good use. The technique works perfectly when you're creating a hat as the shaping flows so naturally you don't even see it.

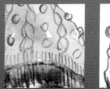

cable wristlets

These sweet hand warmers feature a lovely lace-up detail at the side that makes them both eye-catching and adjustable.

YOU WILL NEED

Artyarns Silk Rhapsody (100% silk core, wrapped in 70% mohair/30% silk; 3.5oz/100g = 260yd/234m): 1 skein, color gray/blue #149—approx 260yd/234m of worsted weight yarn  (A)

Artyarns Ultramerino 4 (100% merino wool; 1.75 oz/50g = 191yd/172m): 1 skein, color gray/blue #149—approx 191yd/172m of sport weight yarn (B)

Artyarns Regal Silk (100% silk; 1.75oz/50g = 163yd/147m): (C) 1 skein, color slate blue #229; (D) 1 skein, color teal #230—approx 326yd/294m of light worsted weight yarn

Artyarns Supermerino (100% merino wool; 1.75oz/50g = 104yd/94m): 1 skein, color blue green #255—approx 104yd/94m of worsted weight yarn (E)

Artyarns Ultramerino 8 (100% merino wool; 3.5oz/100g = 188yd/169m): 1 skein, color teal #230—approx 188yd/169m of worsted weight yarn (F)

Artyarns Silk Mohair Glitter (60% super kid mohair, 40% silk; 0.88oz/25g = 312yd/281m): 1 skein, color blue/silver—approx 312yd/281m of lace weight yarn (G)

NOTE: Only partial balls of each color are required for this project.

Knitting needles: 5mm (size 8 U.S.) *or size to obtain gauge*

Cable needle

Stitch markers

¼"/5mm wide ribbon, 2yd/2m

Tapestry needle

GAUGE

18 sts and 27 rows = 4"/10cm in 1x1 rib using F

Always take time to check your gauge.

SPECIAL ABBREVIATIONS

TW 4L: Sl 3 sts to cn and hold to front of work, (with G) p1, (with F) k3 from cn.

TW 4R: Sl 1 st to cn and hold to back of work, (with F) k3, (with G) p1 from cn.

C6F: Sl 3 sts to cn and hold in front of work, k3, k3 sts from cn.

SKILL LEVEL
Experienced

SIZE
Women's

FINISHED MEASUREMENTS
7 x 7"/18 x 18cm, blocked, before lacing up

RIGHT WRISTLET

Using A, CO 36 sts.

Rows 1 & 3 (WS): Purl.

Row 2: Knit.

Row 4: Sl 1, *k2tog, yo, rep from * to last st, k1.

Rows 5 & 7: Purl.

Row 6: Knit.

Row 8: Pick up a corresponding st of CO row and knit tog with every st on needle to form hem.

Row 9 and every following WS row: Sl 1, p1, [k1, p1] 9 times, k2, p6, k2, [p1, k1] 3 times.

Row 10 (RS): Sl 1, [k1, p1] 2 times, k1, p2, C6F, p2, k1, [p1, k1] 9 times, k1.

Change to 2 strands of B held double.

Rows 12 & 14 (RS): Sl 1, [k1, p1] 2 times, k1, p2, k6, p2, k1, [p1, k1] 9 times, k1.

Row 16 (change to C): Sl 1, [k1, p1] 2 times, k1, p2, k6, p2, k1, [p1, k1] 9 times, k1.

Row 18: Rep row 10.

Row 20 (change to D): Sl 1, [k1, p1] 2 times, k1, p2, k6, p2, k1, [p1, k1] 9 times, k1.

Row 22 (change to E): Sl 1, [k1, p1] 2 times, k1, p2, k6, p2, k1, [p1, k1] 9 times, k1.

Row 24: Rep row 10.

Row 26 (RS): Sl 1, [k1, p1] 2 times, k1, p2, k6, p2, [k1, p1] 2 times, PM, yo, k1, yo, PM, [p1, k1] 7 times, k1.

Row 27: As every WS row, but knit sts between markers.

Row 28 (RS): Sl 1, [k1, p1] 2 times, k1, p2, k6, p2, [k1, p1] 2 times, slip marker, yo, knit sts between markers, yo, slip marker, [p1, k1] 7 times, k1.

Row 30 (RS): Sl 1, [k1, p1] 2 times, k1, p2, C6F, p2, [k1, p1] 2 times, slip marker, yo, knit sts between markers, yo, slip marker, [p1, k1] 7 times, k1.

Rows 32 & 34: Rep row 28.

Row 36: Rep row 30.

Row 38 (RS): Sl 1, [k1, p1] 2 times, k1, p2, k6, p2, [k1, p1] 2 times, remove marker, BO 15 sts between markers, remove marker, [p1, k1] 7 times, k1.

Row 39: [P1, k1] 11 times, p1, CO 5 sts, [k1, p1] twice, k2, p6, k2, [p1, k1] 3 times—40 sts.

Row 40: Sl 1, [k1, p1] 2 times, k1, p2, k6, p2, k1, [p1, k1] 11 times, k1.

Row 41: [P1, k1] 11 times, p1, k2, p6, k2, [p1, k1] 3 times.

Change to F.

Row 42: Sl 1, [k1, p1] 2 times, k1, p2, C6F, p2, k1, [p1, k1] 11 times, k1.

Row 43: [P1, k1] 11 times, p1, k2, p6, k2, [p1, k1] 3 times.

Row 44: Sl 1, [k1, p1] 2 times, k1, p1, TW 4R, TW 4L, p1, k1, [p1, k1] 11 times, k1.

Row 45: (With F) [p1, k1] 11 times, p1, k1, p3, (with G) k2, (with F) p3, k1, [p1, k1] 3 times.

Row 46: (With F) sl 1, [k1, p1] 2 times, k1, TW 4R, (with G) p2, TW 4L, (with F) k1, [p1, k1] 11 times, k1.

Row 47: (With F) [p1, k1] 11 times, p4, (with G) k4, (with F) p4, k1, [p1, k1] 2 times.

Row 48: (With F) sl 1, [k1, p1] 2 times, TW 4R, (with G) p4, TW 4L, (with F) [p1, k1] 11 times, k1.

Row 49: (With F) [p1, k1] 11 times, p3, (with G) k6, (with F) p3, k1, [p1, k1] 2 times.

Row 50: (With F) sl 1, k1, p1, k1, TW 4R, (with G) p6, TW 4L, (with F) [k1, p1] 10 times, k2.

Row 51: (With F) [p1, k1] 10 times, p4, (with G) k8, (with F) p4, k1, p1, k1.

Row 52: (With F) sl 1, k1, p1, TW 4R, (with G) p8, TW 4L, (with F) [p1, k1] 10 times, k1.

Row 53: (With F) [p1, k1] 10 times, p3, (with G) k10, (with F) p3, k1, p1, k1. BO all sts in F in established pattern.

LEFT WRISTLET

Using A, CO 36 sts.

Rows 1 & 3 (WS): Purl.

Row 2: Knit.

Row 4: Sl 1, *k2tog, yo, rep from * to last st, k1.

Rows 5 & 7: Purl.

Row 6: Knit.

Row 8: Pick up a corresponding st of CO row and knit tog with every st on needle to form hem.

Row 9 and every following WS row: Sl 1, p1, [k1, p1] 2 times, k2, p6, k2, [p1, k1] 10 times.

Row 10 (RS): Sl 1, [k1, p1] 9 times, k1, p2, C6F, p2, k1, [p1, k1] 2 times, k1.

Rows 12 & 14 (RS): Sl 1, [k1, p1] 9 times, k1, p2, k6, p2, k1, [p1, k1] 2 times, k1.

Row 16 (change to C): Sl 1, [k1, p1] 9 times, k1, p2, k6, p2, k1, [p1, k1] 2 times, k1.

Row 18: Rep row 10.

Row 20 (change to D): Sl 1, [k1, p1] 9 times, k1, p2, k6, p2, k1, [p1, k1] 2 times, k1.

Row 22: Sl 1, [k1, p1] 9 times, k1, p2, k6, p2, k1, [p1, k1] 2 times, k1.

Row 24: Rep row 10.

These hand warmers were an exercise in problem solving. The challenge was how to make them on a straight needle without having an awkward seam on the side. It was then that I had the lace-up ribbon idea, which allowed me to avoid a seam while at the same time introducing a decorative element.

Row 26 (RS): Sl 1, [k1, p1] 7 times, PM, yo, k1, yo, PM, [p1, k1] 2 times, p2, k6, p2, k1, [p1, k1] 2 times, k1.

Row 27: As every WS row, but knit sts between markers.

Row 28 (RS): Sl 1, [k1, p1] 7 times, slip marker, yo, knit sts between markers, yo, slip marker, [p1, k1] 2 times, p2, k6, p2, k1, [p1, k1] 2 times, k1.

Row 30 (RS): Sl 1, [k1, p1] 7 times, slip marker, yo, knit sts between markers, yo, slip marker, [p1, k1] 2 times, p2, C6F, p2, k1, [p1, k1] 2 times, k1.

Rows 32 & 34: Rep row 28.

Row 36: Rep row 30.

Row 38: Sl 1, [k1, p1] 7 times, remove marker, BO 15 sts between markers, remove marker, k1, p1, k1, p2, k6, p2, k1, [p1, k1] 2 times, k1.

Row 39: [P1, k1] 2 times, p1, k2, p6, k2, [p1, k1] 2 times, CO 5 sts, [k1, p1] 7 times, k1–40 sts.

Row 40: Sl 1, [k1, p1] 11 times, k1, p2, k6, p2, k1, [p1, k1] 2 times, k1.

Row 41: [P1, k1] 2 times, p1, k2, p6, k2, [p1, k1] 12 times.

Change to F.

Row 42: Sl 1, [k1, p1] 11 times, k1, p2, C6F, p2, k1, [p1, k1] 2 times, k1.

Row 43: [P1, k1] 2 times, p1, k2, p6, k2, [p1, k1] 12 times.

Row 44: Sl 1, [k1, p1] 11 times, k1, p1, TW 4R, TW 4L, p1, k1, [p1, k1] 2 times, k1.

Row 45: (With F) [p1, k1] 2 times, p1, k1, p3, (with G) k2, (with F) p3, k1, [p1, k1] 12 times.

Row 46: (With F) sl 1, [k1, p1] 11 times, k1, TW 4R, (with G) p2, TW 4L, (with F) k1, [p1, k1] 2 times, k1.

Row 47: (With F) [p1, k1] 2 times, p4, (with G) k4, (with F) p4, k1, [p1, k1] 11 times.

Row 48: (With F) sl 1, [k1, p1] 11 times, TW 4R, (with G) p4, TW 4L, (with F) [p1, k1] 2 times, k1.

Row 49: (With F) [p1, k1] 2 times, p3, (with G) k6, (with F) p3, k1, [p1, k1] 11 times.

Row 50: (With F) Sl 1, [k1, p1] 10 times, k1, TW 4R, (with G) p6, TW 4L, (with F) k1, p1, k2.

Row 51: (With F) p1, k1, p4, (with G) k8, (with F) p4, k1, [p1, k1] 10 limes.

Row 52: (With F) sl 1, [k1, p1] 10 times, TW 4R, (with G) p8, TW 4L, (with F) p1, k2.

Row 53: (With F) p1, k1, p3, (with G) k10, (with F) p3, k1, [p1, k1] 10 times. BO all sts in F in established pattern.

FINISHING

Weave in ends. Cut ribbon into two equal pieces, lace through slipped sts on sides of armwarmers, and tie in a bow.

cable throw

A traditional cable blanket gets an untraditional edging detail; knitted on afterwards, the trim has lace inserts for a touch of contrast and color.

YOU WILL NEED

Lorna's Laces Shepherd Bulky
(100% superwash wool; 3.5oz/100g
= 140yd/126m): 15 skeins, color
natural #0—approx 2100yd/1890m
of bulky weight yarn (5) (A)

Lorna's Laces Helen's Lace
(50% silk, 50% wool; 4oz/114g
= 1250yd/1125m): 1 skein,
color sand ridge #112—approx
1250yd/1125m of lace weight yarn
(0) (B)

Knitting needles: 6mm (size 10
U.S.) or size to obtain gauge

Cable needle

Bobbins

Stitch markers

Tapestry needle

SKILL LEVEL
Experienced

SIZE
One size

FINISHED MEASUREMENTS
**50 x 68"/127 x 173cm,
blocked, including
the border**

GAUGE

18 sts and 28 rows = 4"/10cm in Cable I

Always take time to check your gauge.

SPECIAL ABBREVIATIONS

M1p: Increase by picking up a bar between 2 sts, twisting and purling it.

3-st TWR: Sl 1 st to cn and hold to back of work, k2, p1 from cn.

3-st TWL: Sl 2 sts to cn and hold to front of work, p1, k2 from cn.

4-st TWR: Sl 1 st to cn and hold to back of work, k3, p1 from cn.

4-st TWL: Sl 3 sts to cn and hold to front of work, p1, k3 from cn.

C4R: Sl 2 sts to cn and hold to back of work, k2, k2 from cn.

C4L: Sl 2 sts to cn and hold to front of work, k2, k2 from cn.

C6R: Sl 3 sts to cn and hold to back of work, k3, k3 from cn.

C6L: Sl 3 sts to cn and hold to front of work, k3, k3 from cn.

TW 4L: Sl 3 sts to cn and hold to front of work, (with B) p1, (with A) k3 from cn.

TW 4R: Sl 1 st to cn and hold to back of work, (with A) k3, (with B) p1 from cn.

PATTERN STITCHES

Cable I (multiple of 6 sts):

Rows 1, 3, & 5 (WS): Purl 6.

Rows 2 & 4: Knit 6.

Row 6: C6L.

Row 7: Purl 6.

Row 8: Knit 6.

Rep rows 1–8 for pattern.

Cable II (multiple of 20 sts):

Row 1 (WS): K4, [p4, k4] twice.

Row 2: P3, [3-st TWR, 3-st TWL, p2] twice, p1.

Rows 3 & 5: K3, [p2, k2] 3 times, p2, k3.

Row 4: P3, [k2, p2] 4 times, p1.

Row 6: P3, [3-st TWL, 3-st TWR, p2] twice, p1.

Rows 7 & 9: K4, [p4, k4] twice.

Row 8: P4, [C4R, p4] twice.

Row 10: P3, [3-st TWR, 3-st TWL, p2] twice, p1.

Row 11: K3, [p2, k2] 4 times, k1.

Row 12: P2, [3-st TWR, p2, 3-st TWL] twice, p2.

Row 13: K2, p2, k4, p4, k4, p2, k2.

Row 14: P1, 3-st TWR, p4, C4L, p4, 3-st TWL, p1.

Row 15: K1, p2, k5, p4, k5, p2, k1.

Row 16: 3-st TWR, p4, 3-st TWR, 3-st TWL, p4, 3-st TWL.

Rows 17 & 19: P2, k5, p2, k2, p2, k5, p2.

Row 18: K2, p5, k2, p2, k2, p5, k2.

Row 20: 3-st TWL, p4, 3-st TWL, 3-st TWR, p4, 3-st TWR.

Row 21: K1, p2, k5, p4, k5, p2, k1.

Row 22: P1, 3-st TWL, p4, C4L, p4, 3-st TWR, p1.

Row 23: K2, p2, k4, p4, k4, p2, k2.

Row 24: P2, [3-st TWL, p2, 3-st TWR] twice, p2.

Row 25: K3, [p2, k2] 4 times, k1.

Row 26: P3, 3-st TWL, 3-st TWR, p2, 3-st TWL, 3-st TWR, p3.

Row 27: K4, [p4, k4] twice.

Row 28: P4, [C4R, p4] twice.

Rep rows 1–28 for pattern.

Cable III (multiple of 44 sts):

Row 1 (WS): K4, [p6, k4] 4 times.

Row 2: P3, [4-st TWR, 4-st TWL, p2] 4 times, p1.

Rows 3 & 5: K3, [p3, k2] 8 times, k1.

Row 4: P3, [k3, p2] 8 times, p1.

Row 6: P3, [4-st TWL, 4-st TWR, p2] 4 times, p1.

Rows 7 & 9: K4, [p6, k4] 4 times.

Row 8: P4, [C6R, p4] 4 times.

Row 10: P3, [4-st TWR, 4-st TWL, p2] 4 times, p1.

Row 11: K3, [p3, k2] 8 times, k1.

Row 12: P2, [4-st TWR, p2, 4-st TWL] 4 times, p2.

Row 13: K2, p3, k4, [p6, k4] 3 times, p3, k2.

Row 14: P1, 4-st TWR, [p4, C6L] 3 times, p4, 4-st TWL, p1.

Row 15: K1, p3, k5, [p6, k4] twice, p6, k5, p3, k1.

Row 16: 4-st TWR, p4, [4-st TWR, 4-st TWL, p2] 3 times, p2, 4-st TWL.

Rows 17 & 19: P3, k5, [p3, k2] 6 times, k3, p3.

Row 18: K3, p5, [k3, p2] 6 times, p3, k3.

Row 20: 4-st TWL, p4, [4-st TWL, 4-st TWR, p2] 3 times, p2, 4-st TWR.

Row 21: K1, p3, k5, [p6, k4] 3 times, k1, p3, k1.

Row 22: P1, 4-st TWL, p4, [C6L, p4] 3 times, 4-st TWR, p1.

Row 23: K2, p3, k4, [p6, k4] 3 times, p3, k2.

Row 24: P2, [4-st TWL, p2, 4-st TWR] 4 times, p2.

Row 25: K3, [p3, k2] 8 times, k1.

Row 26: P3, [4-st TWL, 4-st TWR, p2] 4 times, p1.

Row 27: K4, [p6, k4] 4 times.

Row 28: P4, [C6R, p4] 4 times.

Rep rows 1–28 for Cable III.

instructions

BLANKET

Using A, CO 172 sts.

Row 1 (WS): Sl 1, [work Cable I, p1, work Cable II, p1] twice, work cable I, p1, work Cable III, [p1, work Cable I, p1, work Cable II] twice, p1, work Cable I, p1.

Row 2: Sl 1, [work Cable I, k1, work Cable II, k1] twice, work Cable I, k1, work Cable III, [k1, work Cable I, k1, work Cable II] twice, k1, work Cable I, k1.

Work these two rows for 14 Cable II and Cable III pattern repeats, and 49 Cable I repeats—392 rows.

Work for 5 more rows in all cable patterns, BO on the next row.

BORDER

Mark every Cable I and center 6 sts of Cable III (7 total) on CO edge.

Starting on the RS of work:

Pick up and knit 1 edge st, [pick up and knit 6 Cable I sts, pick up and purl 22 sts to the next Cable I] 6 times, pick up and knit 6 Cable I sts, pick up and knit 1 edge st. (176 sts)

Row 1 (WS): Sl 1, *p6, k22; rep from * to last 7 sts, p7.

Row 2: Sl 1, *C6L, p22; rep from * to last 7 sts, C6L, k1.

Row 3: Rep row 1.

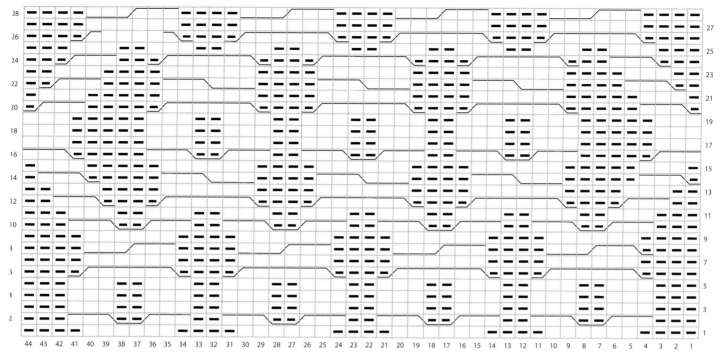

Chart III

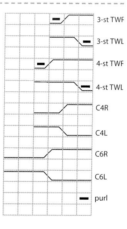

NOTE: Continue working with A and add B as directed. Use bobbins to help manage yarns.

Chart Key

3-st TWF
3-st TWL
4-st TWF
4-st TWL
C4R
C4L
C6R
C6L
purl

Row 4: (With A) sl 1, k3, (with B) M1p, [(with A/B) TW 4L, (with A) p20, (with A/B) TW 4R] to last 4 sts, (with B) M1p, (with A) k4.

Row 5: (With A) sl 1, p3, *(with B) k2, (with A) p3, k20, p3; rep from *, end (with B) k2, (with A) p4.

Row 6: (With A) sl 1, k3, (with B) M1p, p2, [(with A/B) TW 4L, (with A) p18, (with A/B) TW 4R, (with B) p2] to last 4 sts, (with B) M1p, (with A) k4.

Row 7: (With A) sl 1, p3, *(with B) k4, (with A) p3, k18, p3; rep from *, end (with B) k4, (with A) p4.

Row 8: (With A) sl 1, k3, (with B) M1p, p4, [(with A/B) TW 4L, (with A) p16, (with A/B) TW 4R, (with B) p4] to last 4 sts, (with B) M1p, (with A) k4.

Row 9: (With A) sl 1, p3, *(with B) k6, (with A) p3, k16, p3; rep from *, end (with B) k6, (with A) p4.

Row 10: (With A) sl 1, k3, (with B) M1p, p6, [(with A/B) TW 4L, (with A) p14, (with A/B) TW 4R, (with B) p6] to last 4 sts, (with B) M1p, (with A) k4.

Row 11: (With A) sl 1, p3, *(with B) k8, (with A) p3, k14, p3; rep from *, end (with B) k8, (with A) p4.

Row 12: (With A) sl 1, k3, (with B) M1p, p8, [(with A/B) TW 4L, (with A) p12, (with A/B) TW 4R, (with B) p8] to last 4 sts, (with B) M1p, (with A) k4.

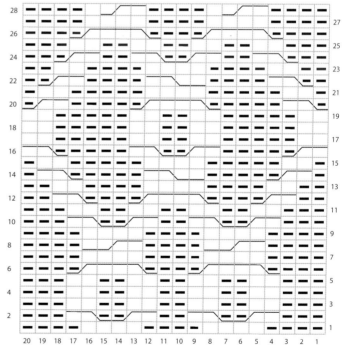

Chart II

Row 13: (With A) sl 1, p3, *(with B) k10, (with A) p3, k12, p3; rep from *, end (with B) k10, (with A) p4.

Row 14: (With A) sl 1, k3, (with B) M1p, p10, [(with A/B) TW 4L, (with A) p10, (with A/B) TW 4R, (with B) p10] to last 4 sts, (with B) M1p, (with A) k4.

Row 15: (With A) sl 1, p3, *(with B) k12, (with A) p3, k10, p3; rep from *, end (with B) k12, (with A) p4.

Row 16: (With A) sl 1, k3, (with B) M1p, p12, [(with A/B) TW 4L, (with A) p8, (with A/B) TW 4R, (with B) p12] to last 4 sts, (with B) M1p, (with A) k4.

Row 17: (With A) sl 1, p3, *(with B) k14, (with A) p3, k8, p3; rep from *, end (with B) k14, (with A) p4.

Row 18: (With A) sl 1, k3, (with B) M1p, p14, [(with A/B) TW 4L, (with A) p6, (with A/B) TW 4R, (with B) p14] to last 4 sts, (with B) M1p, (with A) k4.

Row 19: (With A) sl 1, p3, *(with B) k16, (with A) p3, k6, p3; rep from *, end (with B) k16, (with A) p4.

Row 20: (With A) sl 1, k3, (with B) M1p, p16, [(with A/B) TW 4L, (with A) p4, (with A/B) TW 4R, (with B) p16] to last 4 sts, (with B) M1p, (with A) k4.

Row 21: (With A) sl 1, p3, *(with B) k18, (with A) p3, k4, p3; rep from *, end (with B) k18, (with A) p4.

Row 22: (With A) sl 1, k3, (with B) M1p, p18, [(with A/B) TW 4L, (with A) p2, (with A/B) TW 4R, (with B) p18] to last 4 sts, (with B) M1p, (with A) k4.

Row 23: (With A) sl 1, p3, *(with B) k20, (with A) p3, k2, p3; rep from *, end (with B) k20, (with A) p4.

Row 24: (With A) sl 1, k3, (with B) M1p, p20, [(with A/B) TW 4L, (with A/B) TW 4R, (with B) p20] to last 4 sts, (with B) M1p, (with A) k4.

Row 25: (With A) sl 1, p3, *(with B) k22, (with A) p6; rep from *, end (with B) k22, (with A) p4.

Row 26: (With A) sl 1, k3, *(with B) p22, (with A) C6L; rep from * to last 26 sts, (with B) p22, (with A) k4.

Row 27: Rep row 25.

Next row, (with A/B) BO in pattern.

Rep rows 1–27 for BO edge.

SIDES

Pick up in the same manner for the sides, but be careful to space out sts evenly since there are no cables to match:

Pick up and knit 1 edge st, [pick up and knit 6 sts, pick up and purl 22 sts] 8 times, pick up and knit 6 sts, pick up and knit 1 edge st. (232 sts)

Work rows 1-27 of Border pattern for both sides of the blanket.

FINISHING

Sew corners of border, and weave in ends. Block.

Before I started working on this blanket, I was envisioning a bulky cream-colored piece with a lot of cables and a delicate openwork border. The border is what really makes this piece unique in comparison to other cable blankets.

With asymmetrical cable shaping, the lacy neckline creates a fashionable interplay between what is revealed and what remains concealed.

deep V sweater

YOU WILL NEED

Artyarns Cashmere 3
(100% cashmere; 1.75oz/50g = 170yd/153m): 7 (8, 9) skeins, color olive green #261—approx 1190 (1360, 1530)yd/1071 (1224, 1377)m of light worsted weight yarn (3) (A)

Artyarns Cashmere 1
(100% cashmere; 1.75oz/50g = 510yd/459m): 1 skein, color olive green #261—approx 510yd/459m of fingering weight yarn (1) (B)

Artyarns Beaded Cashmere
(100% cashmere; 1.75oz/50g = 115yd/104m): 1 skein, color olive green #261G—approx 115yd/104m of light worsted weight yarn (3) (C)

Knitting needles: 4 mm (size 6 U.S.) *or size to obtain gauge*

Crochet hook: 3.75mm (size F U.S.)

Cable needle

Tapestry needle

SKILL LEVEL
Experienced

SIZE
Women's S (M, L)

FINISHED MEASUREMENTS
Bust: 36 (40, 44)"/91.5 (101.5, 112)cm

Length: 22 (23½, 25)"/56 (60, 64)cm long, from shorter side

GAUGE
27 sts and 24 rows = 4"/10cm in Cable stitch
Always take time to check your gauge.

SPECIAL ABBREVIATIONS

M1p: Increase by picking up a bar between 2 sts, twisting and purling it.

C6F: Sl 3 sts to cn and hold in front of work, k3, k3 from cn.

C4F: Sl 2 sts to cn and hold in front of work, k2, k2 from cn.

C2F: Sl 1 st to cn and hold in front of work, k1, k1 from cn.

TW 4L: Sl 3 sts to cn and hold to front of work, (with B) p1, (with A) k3 from cn.

TW 4R: Sl 1 st to cn and hold to back of work, (with A) k3, (with B) p1 from cn.

TW 5L: Sl 3 sts to cn and hold to front of work, (with B) p2, (with A) k3 from cn.

TW 5R: Sl 2 sts to cn and hold to back of work, (with A) k3, (with B) p2 from cn.

instructions

BACK

Using A, CO 8 sts.

Rows 1 & 3 (WS): Sl 1, purl to end.

Rows 2 & 4: Sl 1, knit to end.

Row 5: Sl 1, purl to end and CO 7 sts—15 sts.

Row 6: Sl 1, k6, *p1, C6F; rep from * to last st, k1.

Row 7: Sl 1, *p6, k1; rep from * to last 7 sts, p7.

Row 8: Sl 1, k6, *p1, k6; rep from * to last st, k1.

Rows 9 & 10: Rep rows 7 & 8.

Rep rows 5-10 until there are 17 (19, 21) cables—120 (134, 148) sts.

Work even in cable pattern until the shorter side measures 13 (14, 15)"/33 (36, 38)cm.

ARMHOLE SHAPING:

On the following Cable Row 2:

Row 2: BO 3 sts at beg of row, continue in established pattern—117 (131, 145) sts.

Row 3: BO 3 sts at beg of row, work to last 2 sts, k2tog—113 (127, 141) sts.

Rows 4 & 5: BO 2 sts at beg of row, work to last 2 sts, k2tog—107 sts.

Rows 6 & 7: BO 1 st at beg of row, work to last 2 sts, k2tog—103 (121, 135) sts.

Mark center cable by placing markers before and after the cable (6 sts between markers).

Row 8 (pattern row 2): Work to 1 st before the 1st marker, move marker, TW 4R (with A/B), TW 4L (with A/B), move marker, work to last 2 sts in A, k2tog—102 (120, 134) sts.

Row 9: Knit all knit sts and purl all purl sts; work in A where there is A, and B between the markers where there is B.

Row 10: Sl 1, k2tog, work to 2 sts before the 1st marker, move marker, TW 5R (with A/B), purl in B to 3 sts before the marker, TW 5L (with A/B), move marker, work to last 3 sts in A, ssk, k1—100 (118, 132) sts.

Rep rows 9 & 10 until there are 5 (8, 12) sts outside the markers remaining.

Next RS row: Sl 1, k2tog, knit to the marker, (with A) k3, purl in B to 3 sts before the second marker, (with A) k3, knit to last 3 sts, ssk, k1.

Next row: Work sts as established.

Rep last 2 rows 3 (4, 5) more times or until armhole measures 9 (9½, 10)"/23 (24, 25.5)cm.

BO.

FRONT

Using A, CO 8 sts.

Rows 1 & 3 (WS): Sl 1, purl to end.

Row 2: Sl 1, knit to end.

Row 4: Sl 1, knit to end and CO 7 sts—15 sts.

Rows 5 & 7: Sl 1, *p6, k1; rep from * to last 7 sts, p7.

Row 6: Sl 1, *C6F, p1; rep from * to last 7 sts, k7.

Row 8: Sl 1, k6, *p1, k6; rep from * to last st, k1.

Row 9: Sl 1, *p6, k1; rep from * to last 7 sts, p7.

Rep rows 4-9 until there are 17 (19, 21) cables.

Work as for back to the end.

SLEEVES (MAKE 2)

Using A, CO 50 (57, 64) sts.

Row 1 (WS): Purl.

Row 2: Sl 1, k6, *p1, k6; rep from * to last st, k1.

Row 3: Sl 1, p6, *k1, p6; rep from * to last st, p1.

Work Cable I:

Row 1: Sl 1, C6F, *p1, C6F; rep from * to last st, k1.

Rows 2, 4, & 6: Sl 1, p6, *k1, p6; rep from * to last st, p1.

Rows 3 & 5: Sl 1, k6, *p1, k6; rep from * to last st, k1.

Rep rows 1-6 four times (24 rows).

Work Cable II:

Row 1: Sl 1, M1p, PM, C6F, *p1, C6F; rep from * to last st, PM, M1p, k1.

Row 2: Sl 1, k1, p6, *k1, p6; rep from * to last 2 sts, k1, p1.

Row 3: Sl 1, M1, p1, k6, *p1, k6; rep from * to last 2 sts, p1, M1, k1.

Row 4: Sl 1, p1, k1, p6, *k1, p6; rep from * to last 3 sts, k1, p2.

Row 5: Sl 1, M1, k1, p1, k6, *p1, k6; rep from * to last 3 sts, p1, k1, M1, k1–56 (63, 70) sts.

Row 6: Sl 1, p2, k1, p6, *k1, p6; rep from * to last 4 sts, k1, p3.

Work Cable III:

Row 1: Sl 1, C2F, p1, C6F, *p1, C6F; rep from * to last st, p1, C2F, k1.

Row 2: Sl 1, p2, k1, p6, *k1, p6; rep from * to last 4 sts, k1, p3.

Row 3: Sl 1, M1, k2, p1, k6, *p1, k6; rep from * to last 4 sts, p1, k2, M1, k1.

Row 4: Sl 1, p3, k1, p6, *k1, p6; rep from * to last 5 sts, k1, p4.

Row 5: Sl 1, M1, k3, p1, k6, *p1, k6; rep from * to last 5 sts, p1, k3, M1, k1–60 (67, 74) sts.

Row 6: Sl 1, p4, k1, p6, *k1, p6; rep from * to last 6 sts, k1, p5.

Work Cable IV:

Row 1: Sl 1, C4F, p1, C6F, *p1, C6F; rep from * to last 6 sts, p1, C4F, k1.

Rows 2, 4, & 6: Sl 1, p4, k1, p6, *k1, p6; rep from * to last 6 sts, k1, p5.

Rows 3 & 5: Sl 1, k4, p1, k6, *p1, k6; rep from * to last 6 sts, p1, k5.

Rep last 6 rows twice more.

Work Cable V:

Row 1: Sl 1, C4F, p1, C6F, *p1, C6F; rep from * to last 6 sts, p1, C4F, k1.

Row 2: Sl 1, p2, k1, p6, *k1, p6; rep from * to last 4 sts, k1, p3.

Row 3: Sl 1, M1, k4, p1, k6, *p1, k6; rep from * to last 6 sts, p1, k4, M1, k1.

Row 4: Sl 1, p5, k1, p6, *k1, p6; rep from * to last 7 sts, k1, p6.

Row 5: Sl 1, M1, k5, p1, k6, *p1, k6; rep from * to last 7 sts, p1, k5, M1, k1–64 (71, 78) sts.

Row 6: Sl 1, p6, k1, p6, *k1, p6; rep from * to last 8 sts, k1, p7.

Rep Cable I three times more.

Work Cable VI:

Row 1: Sl 1, M1p, PM, C6F, *p1, C6F; rep from * to last st, PM, M1p, k1—66 (73, 80) sts.

Row 2: Sl 1, k1, p6, *k1, p6; rep from * to last 2 sts, k1, p1.

Rows 3 & 5: Sl 1, p1, k6, *p1, k6; rep from * to last 2 sts, p1, k1.

Rows 4 & 6: Sl 1, k1, p6, *k1, p6; rep from * to last 2 sts, k1, p1.

Work Cable VII:

Row 1: Sl 1, p1, C6F, *p1, C6F; rep from * to last 2 sts, p1, k1.

Row 2: Sl 1, k1, p6, *k1, p6; rep from * to last 2 sts, k1, p1.

Rows 3 & 5: Sl 1, p1, k6, *p1, k6; rep from * to last 2 sts, p1, k1.

Rows 4 & 6: Sl 1, k1, p6, *k1, p6; rep from * to last 2 sts, k1, p1.

Rep last 6 rows until sleeve measures 17 (17½, 18)"/43 (44.5, 46)cm, ending with a WS row.

CAP SHAPING:

Row 1 (RS): BO 3 sts at beg of row, continue in established pattern—63 (70, 77) sts.

Row 2: BO 3 sts at beg of row, work to last 2 sts, k2tog—59 (66, 73) sts.

Rows 3 & 4: BO 2 sts at beg of row, work to last 2 sts, k2tog—53 (60, 67) sts.

Rows 5 & 6: BO 1 st at beg of row, work to last 2 sts, k2tog—49 (56, 63) sts.

Row 7: Work to last 2 sts, k2tog—48 (55, 62) sts.

Work in pattern for 5 more rows.

Next (dec) row (RS): Sl 1, k2tog, work to last 3 sts, ssk, k1—42 (45, 48) sts.

Rep dec row every following RS row 3 (5, 7) times—42 (45, 48) sts.

Rep dec row every 4th row 5 times—32 (35, 38) sts.

Rep dec row every other row 3 times—26 (29, 32) sts.

BO.

FINISHING

Sew shoulder seams. Set in sleeves, and sew sleeve and side seams. With crochet hook and C, work 1 round of sc around neck opening, then 1 round of crab st. Fasten off. Weave in ends.

This is one of the most challenging pieces in this book because I wanted to add two unique elements: angled cable ties on the side and a lace neck insert in a lighter yarn. I was really excited to knit the sweater to see how it would actually turn out. While a sketch is always conceptual, sometimes you have to re-design as you go—the only way to prove if an idea is feasible is to just knit it.

freeform

crochet

Freeform is my understanding of the new crochet, when design happens on the spot, depending on what colors or fibers are in front of you at the moment. Experimenting with shapes, color, and texture, I was amazed by the unpredictable and unlimited possibilities of patterns.

Airy and versatile,
this crocheted tank
is assembled out
of many individual
little squares that are
joined together.

lacy
tank

YOU WILL NEED

Claudia Handpainted Silk Lace
(100% silk; 3.5oz/100g =
1100yd/990m): (A) 1 skein, color
undyed natural; (B) 1 skein, color
marigold; (C) 1 skein, color teal;
(D) 1 skein, color chocolate—
approx 4400yd/3960m of lace
weight yarn

Crochet hook: 2.25mm (size B
U.S.) *or size to obtain gauge*

Tapestry needle

SKILL LEVEL
Intermediate

SIZE
Women's S (M, L)

FINISHED MEASUREMENTS
**Bust: 33 (36, 39)"/84
(91.5, 99)cm**

**Length: 26 (26,
27½)"/66 (66, 70)cm**

GAUGE

One motif = 1½"/4cm

Always take time to check your gauge.

PATTERN STITCHES

Crocheted Motif:

Base:

*Ch 24 and join in a ring with a sl st; rep from * 3 times more, joining all in the same place, as if making petals on a flower—4 ch 24 loops. Fasten off if changing color.

Middle (do not break yarn if working with the same color):

*Ch 18 and join in a ring in the center as before (each smaller loop should fit inside a larger loop); rep from * 3 times more—4 ch 18 loops. Fasten off if changing color.

Top (do not break yarn if working with the same color). This is going to be a circle that connects all the petals:

If working last round in same color, begin by sl st to starting point, 3 chs from center on large loop. If changing color, join new yarn with sl st at starting point, 3 chs from center on large loop.

*Sl st in first leg of large loop, ch 1, sl st in center of first leg of small loop (the loop inside large loop just worked), ch 1, sl st in center of second leg of first small loop, ch 1, sl st in next leg of large loop (3 chs from center as before), ch 1; rep from * around, join with sl st to first sl st. Fasten off.

instructions

FRONT AND BACK

Crochet motifs as follows:

Motif 1:

Using A, make 264 (288, 338) motifs.

Motif 2:

Using A for Base and Middle and B for Top, make 22 (24, 26) motifs.

Motif 3:

Using C for Base, A for Middle and B for Top, make 12 (14, 16) motifs.

Motif 4:

Using C for Base, B for Middle and D for Top, make 22 (24, 26) motifs.

FINISHING

Connect motifs by joining at the corners through the larger loops.

BODY:

Using Motif 1, join in rounds of 22 (24, 26) motifs, with a total of 12 (12, 13) rounds.

On top of Motif 1 body, add a round of Motif 2.

ARMHOLE SHAPING:

Omit 5 motifs on each side for armhole. Using Motif 3, join a row of 6 (7, 8) motifs centered on front and back.

Using Motif 4, join a row of 6 (7, 8) motifs above the Motif 3 row on front and back.

STRAPS:

Using Motif 4, join 1 motif at each edge on front, join 4 more motifs above this one to form straps, leaving center 4 (5, 6) motifs open for neck opening. Join ends of straps to back.

NECKLINE:

Using C and starting at the joint of two motifs, *work 2 sc in 2 chs of large loop, dc in the next 2 ch, ch 3, 2 dc in the 3rd and 4th ch from center, sc in next 2 sts; rep from * around. Work 1 more round of crab st for a decorative edge.

UNDERARM:

Using A and starting at the joint of two motifs, work as follows only for 5 underarm opening motifs: *work 2 sc in 2 chs of large loop, dc in the next 2 ch, ch 3, 2 dc in the 3rd and 4th ch from center, sc in next 2 sts; rep from * for 5 motifs and then work back in crab st for a decorative edge. Rep for opposite underarm.

ARMHOLE:

Using C and starting at the joint of two motifs, work as follows only for 9 armhole side opening motifs: *work 2 sc in 2 chs of large loop, dc in the next 2 ch, ch 3, 2 dc in the 3rd and 4th ch from center, sc in next 2 sts; rep from * for 9 motifs and then work back in crab st for a decorative edge. Rep for opposite armhole.

Weave in ends.

This is the perfect portable project! What I really wanted when I started designing this tank was an accessory that could be layered over an outfit—rather than a garment that would stand on its own—so I came up with an open design.

Beaded flowers and dangling chain loops form your new favorite—and ultra-easy-to-make— fashion accessories.

flower earrings

YOU WILL NEED

30yd/27m flexible fine gauge craft wire

Crochet hook: 2.25mm (size B U.S.) *or size to obtain gauge*

Assorted tiny seed and bugle beads

Ear wires

Needle-nose pliers

Wire cutters

SKILL LEVEL
Easy

SIZE
One size

FINISHED MEASUREMENTS
2 x 5¼"/5 x 13.5cm

A t some time or another, many designers seem to go through a pop art "period"—like Andy Warhol and his factory superstars. These earrings were my take on Edie Sedgwick's style and her out-of-proportion chandelier earrings. Inspired, I decided to design a more delicate, lighter version of them.

GAUGE

20 sts = 4"/10cm in Chain stitch

Always take time to check your gauge.

instructions

EARRING (MAKE 2)

FLOWER:

Prestring 18 bugle beads on the wire first, then 9 seed beads.

With loose end of wire, ch 4 sts and join in a ring with a sl st

Round 1: Work 9 sc into the center opening of the ring, bringing up a seed bead to the front of the work each time before completing the stitch, join with a sl st at the end of round.

Round 2: Dc twice into every sc of previous round, bringing up a bugle bead to the front of the work before beginning each st, join with a sl st at the end of round.

Round 3: *Ch 7, skip 1 dc and sl st into the second dc, ch 5, skip 1 dc and sl st into the second dc, ch 7, skip 2 dcs and sl st into the third dc, ch 5, skip 1 dc and sl st into the second dc; rep from * once more (8 petals made). Set aside.

RAINDROPS (make 3 for each earring):

Prestring 9 seed beads and ch 9 sts, working 1 bead into each chain. Join in ring with sl st, leaving 3"/7.5cm long tail.

Make 2 more rings as before, without beads.

Using pliers, join rings into chains of 3, with beaded ring at the top. Trim excess ends of wire.

FINISHING

Attach 1 raindrop to the bottom petal and to petals on either side.

Attach ear wire to top petal.

butterfly sweater

a simple fitted silhouette—created with stockinette stitch—is the perfect setting for a glamorous detail: a colorful crocheted butterfly insert on the back.

instructions

YOU WILL NEED

Artyarns Cashmere 2 (100% cash-mere; 1.75oz/50g = 255yd/230m): 4 (5, 6) skeins, color peach #128—approx 1020 (1275, 1530) yd/918 (1148, 1377)m of sport weight yarn **(2)** (A)

Short lengths of yarn, in a variety of fibers, colors, and weights, for but-terfly (B-K)

Knitting needles: 3.75mm (size 5 U.S.) *or size to obtain gauge*

Crochet hook: 2.75mm (size C U.S.)

Tapestry needle

SKILL LEVEL
Intermediate

SIZE
Women's S (M, L,)

FINISHED MEASUREMENTS
Bust: 32 (36, 40)"/81.5 (92, 102) cm

Length: 21 (22½, 24)"/53 (57, 61)cm

FRONT

HEM:

Using A, CO 92 (118, 144) sts.

Work in St st for ¾"/2cm, ending with a WS row.

Next row (RS): Purl (to form turning ridge for hem).

Continue in St st for for ¾"/2cm more, ending with a WS row.

Next row (RS): *Pick up a corresponding st of CO row and knit tog with first st on needle; rep from * to end (hem complete).

BODY:

Continue working in St st until piece measures 4¼ (4¾, 4¾)"/11 (12, 12)cm from beg.

WAIST SHAPING:

Next (dec) row (RS): Sl 1, k2tog, knit to last 3 sts, ssk, k1.

Rep dec row every RS row a total of 3 (4, 4) times—86 (110, 136) sts.

Work even in St st for 1 (1, 1½)"/2.5 (2.5, 4)cm.

Next (inc) row (RS): Sl 1, M1, knit to last st, M1, k1.

Rep inc row every RS row a total of 4 (5, 5) times—94 (120, 146) sts.

Work even in St st until piece measures 15 (16, 17)"/38 (41, 43)cm.

ARMHOLE SHAPING:

Row 1 (RS): BO 3 sts at beg of row, continue in established pattern—91 (117, 143) sts.

Row 2: BO 3 sts at beg of row, work to last 2 sts, k2tog—87 (113, 139) sts.

Rows 3 & 4: BO 2 sts at the beg of row, work to last 2 sts, k2tog—81 (107, 133) sts.

For size M only:

Rep rows 3 & 4 twice more—95 sts.

For size L only:

Rep rows 3 & 4 three times more—115 sts.

Rows 5 & 6: BO 1 st at beg of row, work to last 2 sts, k2tog—77 (91, 111) sts.

For size M only:

Rep rows 5 & 6 twice more—83 sts.

For size L only:

Rep rows 5 & 6 three times more—99 sts.

Row 7: Work to last 2 sts, k2tog—76 (82, 98) sts.

Next row: Purl.

Next (dec) row (RS): Sl 1, k2tog, work to last 3 sts, ssk, k1.

Next row: Purl.

Rep last 2 rows until there are 42 (46, 52) sts. BO.

BACK

Work same as for front until piece measures 11½ (12, 12½)"/29 (30.5, 32)cm. Center back shaping:

Work to center 10 sts, join a second ball of yarn, and BO 10 center sts; work to end—42 (55, 68) sts on each side.

Work each side separately as follows:

Next row (RS): Work to last 2 sts, k2tog; on opposite side, ssk, work to end.

Next row (WS): Work to last 2 sts, p2tog; on opposite side, ssp, work to end. Rep last 2 rows until 12 (21, 24) sts remain on each side.

Work even until piece measures 15 (16, 17)"/38 (41, 43)cm, work armhole shaping as follows:

Row 1 (RS): BO 3 sts at beg of row, continue in established pattern; work to end.

Row 2: BO 3 sts at beg of row; work to last 2 sts, k2tog.

Rows 3 & 4: BO 2 sts at beg of row; work to last 2 sts, k2tog.

For size M only:

Rep rows 3 & 4 three times more.

For size L only:

Rep rows 3 & 4 four times more.

Rows 5 & 6: BO 1 st at beg of row; work to last 2 sts, k2tog.

Row 7: Work to the end; work to last 2 sts, k2tog—2 sts left on each side.

Row 8: K2tog; k2tog. Fasten off last st on each side.

SLEEVES

Hem:

Using A, CO 38 (44, 50) sts.

Work hem as for front.

Work even in St st until sleeve measures 3"/8cm, ending with a WS row.

Next (inc) row (RS): Sl 1, M1, work to last st, M1, k1—40 (46, 52) sts.

Rep inc row every following 8th row 10 (11, 12) times—60 (68, 76) sts.

Then work even until sleeve measures 20 (21, 22)"/51 (53, 56)cm.

CAP SHAPING:

Row 1 (RS): BO 3 sts at beg of row, continue in established pattern—57 (65, 73) sts.

Row 2: BO 3 sts at beg of row, work to last 2 sts, k2tog—53 (61, 69) sts.

Rows 3 & 4: BO 2 sts at beg of row, work to last 2 sts, k2tog—47 (55, 63) sts.

Rows 5 & 6: BO 1 st at beg of row, work to last 2 sts, k2tog—43 (51, 59) sts.

For size M only:

Rep rows 5 & 6 once more—47 sts.

For size L only:

Rep rows 5 & 6 twice more—51 sts.

Row 7: Work to last 2 sts, k2tog—42 (46, 50) sts.

Row 8: Purl.

Next (dec) row (RS): Sl 1, k2tog, work to last 3 sts, ssk, k1.

Next row: Purl. Rep last 2 rows until there are 18 (22, 24) sts. Work even for 2"/5cm, BO.

FINISHING

Put sleeves in place and sew along raglan lines. Sew sleeve and side seams. Weave in ends.

Freeform Butterfly:

With crochet hook and using illustration below as a guide, create crocheted chains in different yarns in a variety of lengths, joining each in a ring with a sl st. Gather completed chain loops together and stitch center to gather the "body" of the butterfly. With tapestry needle and A, sew individual loops in place to back opening of sweater to form the "wings" of the butterfly. Tack shorter loops in place on longer loops to secure.

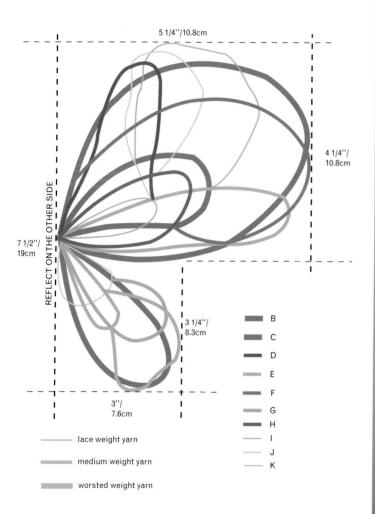

5 1/4''/10.8cm

4 1/4''/10.8cm

REFLECT ON THE OTHER SIDE

7 1/2''/19cm

3 1/4''/8.3cm

3''/7.6cm

	B
	C
	D
	E
	F
	G
	H
	I
	J
	K

lace weight yarn

medium weight yarn

worsted weight yarn

This sweater afforded me the opportunity to really play with freeform crochet. My biggest concern was to avoid over-designing the piece. After multiple sketches, I settled on a very simple stockinette body that would balance out the complicated open work on the back.

Constructed with repeated half moon shapes and multiple weights of the same fiber, this shawl reflects a balance between heavy and light, condensed and delicate.

half moon stole

SKILL LEVEL
Intermediate

SIZE
One size

FINISHED MEASUREMENTS
63"/160cm across top edge, blocked

YOU WILL NEED

Jade Sapphire 12-ply Mongolian Cashmere (100% cashmere; 1.9oz/55g = 70yd/63m): 1 skein, color Robin's Egg blue #19—approx 70yd/63m of chunky weight yarn **5** (A)

Jade Sapphire 8-ply Mongolian Cashmere (100% cashmere; 1.9oz/55g = 100yd/90m): 1 skein, color Robin's Egg blue #19—approx 100yd/90m of worsted weight yarn **4** (B)

Jade Sapphire 6-ply Mongolian Cashmere (100% cashmere; 1.9oz/55g = 150yd/135m): 1 skein, color Robin's Egg blue #19—approx 150yd/135m of DK weight yarn **3** (C)

Jade Sapphire 4-ply Mongolian Cashmere (100% cashmere; 1.9oz/55g = 200yd/180m): 1 skein, color Robin's Egg blue #19—approx 200yd/180m of sport weight yarn **2** (D)

Jade Sapphire 2-ply Mongolian Cashmere (100% cashmere; 1.9oz/55g = 400yd/360m): 1 skein, color Robin's Egg blue #19—approx 400yd/360m of fingering weight yarn **1** (E)

Crochet hook: 2.25mm (size B U.S.) and 3.75mm (size F U.S.) *or size to obtain gauge*

Tapestry needle

One motif = 9"/23cm at widest point & 5"/13cm in height

Always take time to check your gauge.

instructions

HALF MOON I (MAKE 16)

Using smaller hook and A, ch 8 and join in a ring with a sl st.

Row 1: Work 8 sc into center of ring, keeping sts on one side to begin half circle. Cut yarn, fasten off. Do not turn.

Change to B.

Row 2: Join yarn in 1st sc of the previous row and ch 3 (does not count as 1st st, here or throughout), dc in same st. Work 2 dc in each remaining sc across to last 2 sts, dc in last 2 sc—13 dc.

Cut yarn, fasten off. Do not turn.

Change to C.

Row 3: Join yarn at top of ch-3 from previous row, ch 5. *Tr in dc, ch 1; rep from * across—13 tr.

Cut yarn, fasten off. Do not turn.

Change to D.

Row 4: Join yarn at top of ch-5 from previous row, ch 6. *Tr in ch-1 sp (skip 1st tr), ch 1, tr in tr; rep from * across, ending in tr—24 tr.

Cut yarn, fasten off. Do not turn.

Change to E.

Row 5: Join yarn at top of ch-6 from previous row, ch 8.*Dtr in ch-1 sp, ch 1; rep from * across—24 dtr.

Do not cut yarn, turn. Change to larger hook.

Row 6: Ch 6, *tr in ch-1 sp, rep from * across—24 tr.

Turn.

Row 7: Ch 8, tr in 1st ch-1 sp, *2 tr in each ch-1 sp; rep from * to last ch-1 sp, tr—46 tr.

Cut yarn, fasten off.

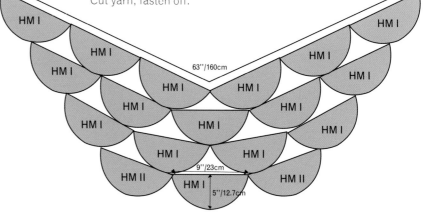

HALF MOON II (MAKE 2)

Work as for Half Moon I through end of row 4. Do not cut yarn, turn.

Row 5: Using E yarn, ch 8, *dtr in ch-1 sp, ch 1; rep from * across—24 dtr.

Turn, change to larger hook.

Row 6: Ch 6, *tr in ch-1 sp, rep from * across—24 tr.

Turn.

Row 7: Ch 6, *tr in ch-1 sp, rep from * across—24 tr.

Cut yarn, fasten off.

FINISHING

Block pieces before assembling. Following diagram, arrange half moons and whipstitch together. Weave in ends.

F reeform crochet can be a little tricky, because even though you have an idea sketched out, it can change multiple times along the way as you discover new possibilities. That's exactly what happened with this shawl. I redesigned the final layout so many times that I just decided to continue crocheting my little half-moon shapes until I had enough of them to turn them into a shawl.

honeycomb

CHAPTER 8

adaptations

Looking at receding shapes in architecture, I decided to shape
the honeycomb pattern by decreasing within the pattern.
I was delighted to watch this pattern—already quite busy—
take a completely different form. For this chapter,
I chose projects that have interesting shapes and
presented three unique ways of using the pattern.

Worked from the top down in a decreasing honeycomb pattern, this top gracefully drapes over the shoulders and transitions into a rib pattern for a chic, fitted bodice.

fitted
blouse

YOU WILL NEED

Artyarns Regal Silk (100% silk; 1.75oz/50g = 163yd/147m): (A) 4 (4, 5) skeins, color dark olive #265; (B) 2 (3, 3) skeins, color light olive #261—approx 978 (1141, 1304)/880 (1027, 1174)m of light worsted weight yarn ③

Knitting needles: 4mm (size 6 U.S.) *or size to obtain gauge*

Crochet hook: 3.25mm (size D U.S.)

Tapestry needle

SKILL LEVEL
Experienced

SIZE
Women's S (M, L)

FINISHED MEASUREMENTS
Bust: 32 (36, 38)"/81 (91.5, 96.5)cm

Length: 25½ (27, 27½)"/65 (69, 70)cm

GAUGE

22 sts and 25 rows = 4"/10cm in 1x1 rib

Always take time to check your gauge.

instructions

PATTERN STITCH

Honeycomb (multiple of 6 + 3 sts):

Row 1 (WS): With A, knit.

Row 2 (RS): With B, k1, *sl 1 wyib, k5, turn; sl 1 wyif, p4, turn; sl 1 wyib, k4, turn; sl 1 wyif, p4, turn; sl 1 wyib, k4; rep from *, end sl 1 wyib, k1.

Row 3: With B, k1, *sl 1 wyif, p5; rep from *, end sl 1 wyif, p1.

Row 4: With A, k1, *k1 tbl, k5; rep from *, end k1 tbl, k1.

Rep rows 1–4 for pattern.

FRONT AND BACK (MAKE 2)

With A, CO 243 (249, 255) sts.

Work 8 (8, 12) rows in Honeycomb pattern—2 (2, 3) pattern repeats.

Next pattern repeat (decreases):

Row 1 (WS): With A, knit.

Row 2 (RS): With B, k1, *sl 1 wyib, k5, turn; sl 1 wyif, p4, turn; sl 1 wyib, k4, turn; sl 1 wyif, p4, turn; sl 1 wyib, k2tog, k2; rep from *, end sl 1 wyib, k1—203 (208, 213) sts.

Row 3: With B, k1, *sl 1 wyif, p4; rep from *, end sl 1 wyif, p1.

Row 4: With A, k1, *k1 tbl, k4; rep from *, end k1 tbl, k1.

Rep last 4 rows 2 (3, 3) times more, but work row 2 as follows:

Row 2 (RS): With B, k1, *sl 1 wyib, k4, turn; sl 1 wyif, p3, turn; sl 1 wyib, k3, turn; sl 1 wyif, p3, turn; sl 1 wyib, k3; rep from *, end sl 1 wyib, k1.

Next pattern repeat (decreases):

Row 1 (WS): With A, knit.

Row 2 (RS): With B, k1, *sl 1 wyib, k4, turn; sl 1 wyif, p3, turn; sl 1 wyib, k3, turn; sl 1 wyif, p3, turn; sl 1 wyib, k2tog, k1; rep from *, end sl 1 wyib, k1—163 (167, 171) sts.

Row 3: With B, k1, *sl 1 wyif, p3; rep from *, end sl 1 wyif, p1.

Row 4: With A, k1, *k1 tbl, k3, rep from *, end k1 tbl, k1.

Rep last 4 rows three times more, but work row 2 as follows:

Row 2 (RS): With B, k1, *sl 1 wyib, k3, turn; sl 1 wyif, p2, turn; sl 1 wyib, k2, turn; sl 1 wyif, p2, turn; sl 1 wyib, k2; rep from *, end sl 1 wyib, k1.

Next pattern repeat (decreases):

Row 1 (WS): With A, knit.

Row 2 (RS): With B, k1, *sl 1 wyib, k3, turn; sl 1 wyif, p2, turn; sl 1 wyib, k2, turn; sl 1 wyif, p2, turn; sl 1 wyib, k2tog; rep from *, end sl 1 wyib, k1—123 (126, 129) sts.

Row 3: With B, k1, *sl 1 wyif, p2; rep from *, end sl 1 wyif, p1.

Row 4: With A, k1, *k1 tbl, k2, rep from *, end k1 tbl, k1.

Next 2 repeats:

Row 1 (WS): With A, knit.

Row 2 (RS): With B, k1, *sl 1 wyib, k2, turn; sl 1 wyif, p1, turn; sl 1 wyib, k1; rep from *, end sl 1 wyib, k1.

Row 3: With B, k1, *sl 1 wyif, p2; rep from *, end sl 1 wyif, p1.

Row 4: With A, k1, *k1 tbl, k2; rep from *, end k1 tbl, k1.

For size S only:

Next pattern repeat (decreases):

Row 1 (WS): With A, knit.

Row 2 (RS): With B, k1, *sl 1 wyib, k2tog; rep from *, end sl 1 wyib, k1–83 sts.

Row 3: With B, k1, *sl 1 wyif, p1; rep from *, end sl 1 wyif, p1.

Row 4: With A, sl 1, p1, *k1, p1; rep from *, end k1.

Row 5: Sl 1, k1, *p1, k1; rep from *, end k1.

For size M only:

Next pattern repeat (decreases):

Row 1 (WS): With A, knit.

Row 2 (RS): With B, k1, *sl 1 wyib, k2tog, sl 1 wyib, k2; rep from *, end sl 1 wyib, k2tog, k1–105 sts.

Row 3: With B, k1, *sl 1 wyif, p1; rep from *, end sl 1 wyif, p1.

Row 4: With A, sl 1, p1, *k1, p1; rep from *, end k1.

Row 5: Sl 1, k1, *p1, k1; rep from *, end k1.

For size L only:

Next pattern repeat (decreases):

Row 1 (WS): With A, knit.

Row 2 (RS): With B, k1, *sl 1 wyib, k2tog, [sl 1 wyib, k2] twice; rep from *, end sl 1 wyib, k1–115 sts.

Row 3: With B, k1, *sl 1 wyif, p1; rep from *, end sl 1 wyif, p1.

Row 4: With A, sl 1, p1, *k1, p1; rep from *, end k1.

Row 5: Sl 1, k1, *p1, k1; rep from *, end k1.

Rep rows 4 and 5 until ribbed portion measures 18 (19, 19)"/46 (48, 48)cm. BO loosely in pattern.

FINISHING

Sew side seams along ribbed portion, leaving remaining part of sides open for armholes.

Sew the cast-on sides of scallop edges: 15 (15, 16) scallops in from each side, leaving the center open for the neckline. With crochet hook and A, sc 90 (96, 102) sts around neck opening. Fasten off.

Weave in ends.

This was an exciting piece to design. Searching for just the right shape and drape, I decided to reverse the pattern and knit the blouse top-down. Gauge is the most important aspect to this piece as you'll get the correct drape and proportion only if the gauge is right.

Decreases in the honeycomb pattern create an elegant scalloped shape for some vintage-inspired sophistication.

scallop purse

SKILL LEVEL
Experienced

SIZE
One size

FINISHED MEASUREMENTS
4½ x 7"/11.5 x 18cm

YOU WILL NEED

Artyarns Beaded Silk (100% silk with beads; 1.75oz/50g = 100yd/90m): 1 skein, color black #246—approx 100yd/90m of light worsted weight yarn (3) (A)

Artyarns Regal Silk (100% silk; 1.75oz/50g = 163yd/147m): (B) 1 skein, color gray #257; (C) 1 skein, color black #246—approx 326yd/293m of light worsted weight yarn (3)

Knitting needles: 3.75mm (size 5 U.S.) needle *or size to obtain gauge*

Crochet hook: 3.75mm (size F U.S.)

16 x 16"/41 x 41cm piece of **lining fabric** (optional)

Sewing needle and thread (if using lining)

4½"/11.5cm wide **purse frame**

Tapestry needle

GAUGE

28 sts and 30 rows = 4"/10cm in St st

Always take time to check your gauge.

instructions

PATTERN STITCH

Honeycomb (multiple of 6 + 3 sts):

Row 1 (WS): With A, knit.

Row 2 (RS): With B, k1, *sl 1 wyib, k5, turn; sl 1 wyif, p4, turn; sl 1 wyib, k4, turn; sl 1 wyif, p4, turn; sl 1 wyib, k4; rep from *, end sl 1 wyib, k1.

Row 3: With B, k1, *sl 1 wyif, p5; rep from *, end sl 1 wyif, p1.

Row 4: With A, k1, *k1 tbl, k5; rep from *, end k1 tbl, k1.

Rep rows 1–4 for pattern.

FRONT AND BACK (MAKE 2)

With A, CO 51 sts.

Work 12 rows in Honeycomb pattern—3 pattern repeats.

Next pattern repeat (decreases):

Row 1 (WS): With A, knit.

Row 2 (RS): With B, k1, *sl 1 wyib, k5, turn; sl 1 wyif, p4, turn; sl 1 wyib, k4, turn; sl 1 wyif, p4, turn; sl 1 wyib, k2tog, k2; rep from *, end sl 1 wyib, k1—43 sts.

Row 3: With B, k1, *sl 1 wyif, p4; rep from *, end sl 1 wyif, p1.

Row 4: With A, k1, *k1 tbl, k4; rep from *, end k1 tbl, k1.

Rep last 4 rows 2 times more, but work row 2 as follows:

  Row 2 (RS): With B, k1, *sl 1 wyib, k4, turn; sl 1 wyif, p3, turn; sl 1 wyib, k3, turn; sl 1 wyif, p3, turn; sl 1 wyib, k3; rep from *, end sl 1 wyib, k1.

  Next pattern repeat (decreases):

  Row 1 (WS): With A, knit.

  Row 2 (RS): With B, k1, *sl 1 wyib, k4, turn; sl 1 wyif, p3, turn; sl 1 wyib, k3, turn; sl 1 wyif, p3, turn; sl 1 wyib, k2tog, k1; rep from *, end sl 1 wyib, k1—35 sts.

  Row 3: With B, k1, *sl 1 wyif, p3; rep from *, end sl 1 wyif, p1.

  Row 4: With A, k1, *k1 tbl, k3; rep from *, end k1 tbl, k1.

  Rep last 4 rows 7 times more, but work row 2 as follows:

    Row 2 (RS): With B, k1, *sl 1 wyib, k3, turn; sl 1 wyif, p2, turn; sl 1 wyib, k2, turn; sl 1 wyif, p2, turn; sl 1 wyib, k2; rep from *, end sl 1 wyib, k1.

Then on the next RS row, switch to C and work in St st for 5 rows.

Row 6: Knit (turning ridge for casing).

Row 7 (RS): Knit.

Work 4 more rows in St st. BO.

FINISHING

If desired, cut lining to fit bag, leaving ½"/1.5cm on all sides for seam allowance. Sew side seams using needle and thread. Fold down top edges of lining, and hem neatly.

Sew the side seams of purse, leaving the top 2"/5cm open for purse frame. Weave in ends.

If used, insert lining in bag with WS together and tack in place neatly.

Fold top casing around purse frame, and sew in place.

With crochet hook and C, work a chain 25"/64cm long, fasten off. Fold in half and attach to purse frame.

Inspired by receding forms in architecture, this purse is a knitting expression of perspective. When I started working on variations of the honeycomb pattern, I knew I wanted something that had a beginning and an end—something that vanished at the point. I achieved my vision when I started decreasing the scallops within the pattern.

peplum cardigan

k Knitted as a single piece without seams, the flared bottom on this cardigan accentuates the waistline for a structured, yet feminine look.

Alpaca Yarn Company Classic Alpaca (100% alpaca; 1.75oz/50g = 110yd/99m): (A) 6 (7, 8) skeins, color light brown #211; (B) 4 (4, 5) skeins, color dark brown #109—approx 1100 (1210, 1430)yd/990 (1089, 1287)m of DK weight yarn ❸

Knitting needles: 4mm (size 6 U.S.) 24"/61cm circular needle *or size to obtain gauge*

Crochet hook: 3.25mm (size D U.S.)

Stitch markers

Stitch holders

¼" (5mm) **velvet ribbon,** 2yd/2m

Tapestry needle

SKILL LEVEL
Experienced

SIZE
Women's S (M, L)

FINISHED MEASUREMENTS
Bust: 33 (39, 41)"/84 (99, 104)cm

Length: 26 (27½, 29)"/66 (70, 74)cm

GAUGE

17 sts and 24 rows = 4"/10cm in St st, blocked

Always take time to check your gauge.

instructions

PATTERN STITCH

Honeycomb (multiple of 6 + 3 sts):

Row 1 (WS): With A, knit.

Row 2 (RS): With B, k1, *sl 1 wyib, k5, turn; sl 1 wyif, p4, turn; sl 1 wyib, k4, turn; sl 1 wyif, p4, turn; sl 1 wyib, k4; rep from *, end sl 1 wyib, k1.

Row 3: With B, k1, *sl 1 wyif, p5; rep from *, end sl 1 wyif, p1.

Row 4: With A, k1, *k1 tbl, k5; rep from *, end k1 tbl, k1.

Rep rows 1–4 for pattern.

- -
NOTE: The fronts and back are knitted in one piece.
- -

BODY

Using A, CO 369 (387, 405) sts. Do not join, work back and forth in rows.

Work in Honeycomb pattern for 4 rows, ending with a RS row.

Next pattern repeat (decreases):

Row 1 (WS): With A, knit.

Row 2 (RS): With B, k1, *sl 1 wyib, k5, turn; sl 1 wyif, p4, turn; sl 1 wyib, k4, turn; sl 1 wyif, p4, turn; sl 1 wyib, k2tog, k2; rep from *, end sl 1 wyib, k1—308 (323, 338) sts.

Row 3: With B, k1, *sl 1 wyif, p4; rep from *, end sl 1 wyif, p1.

Row 4: With A, k1, *k1 tbl, k4; rep from *, end k1 tbl, k1.

Rep last 4 rows one more time, but work row 2 as follows:

Row 2 (RS): With B, k1, *sl 1 wyib, k4, turn; sl 1 wyif, p3, turn; sl 1 wyib, k3, turn; sl 1 wyif, p3, turn; sl 1 wyib, k3; rep from *, end sl 1 wyib, k1.

Next pattern repeat (decreases):

Row 1 (WS): With A, knit.

Row 2 (RS): With B, k1, *sl 1 wyib, k4, turn; sl 1 wyif, p3, turn; sl 1 wyib, k3, turn; sl 1 wyif, p3, turn; sl 1 wyib, k2tog, k1; rep from *, end sl 1 wyib, k1–247 (259, 271) sts.

Row 3: With B, k1, *sl 1 wyif, p3; rep from *, end sl 1 wyif, p1.

Row 4: With A, k1, *k1 tbl, k3; rep from *, end k1 tbl, k1.

Rep last 4 rows one more time, but work row 2 as follows:

Row 2 (RS): With B, k1, *sl 1 wyib, k3, turn; sl 1 wyif, p2, turn; sl 1 wyib, k2, turn; sl 1 wyif, p2, turn; sl 1 wyib, k2; rep from *, end sl 1 wyib, k1.

Next pattern repeat (decreases):

Row 1 (WS): With A, knit.

Row 2 (RS): With B, k1, *sl 1 wyib, k3, turn; sl 1 wyif, p2, turn; sl 1 wyib, k2, turn; sl 1 wyif, p2, turn; sl 1 wyib, k2tog; rep from *, end sl 1 wyib, k–186 (195, 204) sts.

Row 3: With B, k1, *sl 1 wyif, p2; rep from *, end sl 1 wyif, p1.

Row 4: With A, k1, *k1 tbl, k2; rep from *, end k1 tbl, k1.

Next repeat:

Row 1 (WS): With A, knit.

Row 2 (RS): With B, k1, *sl 1 wyib, k2, turn; sl 1 wyif, p1, turn; sl 1 wyib, k1; rep from *, end sl 1 wyib, k1.

Row 3: With B, k1, *sl 1 wyif, p2; rep from *, end sl 1 wyif, p1.

Row 4: With A, k1, *k1 tbl, k2; rep from *, end k1 tbl, k1.

For size S only:

Next pattern repeat (decreases):

Row 1 (WS): With A, knit.

Row 2 (RS): With B, k1, *sl 1 wyib, k2tog; rep from *, end sl 1 wyib, k1–125 sts.

Row 3: With B, k1, *sl 1 wyif, p1; rep from *, end sl 1 wyif, p1.

Row 4: Sl 1, with A, p1, *with B k1, with A p1; rep from *, end with B k1.

Row 5: Sl 1, with A, k1, * with B p1, with A k1; rep from *, end with A k1.

Rep rows 4 & 5 three more times.

For sizes M & L only:

Next pattern repeat (decreases):

Row 1 (WS): With A, knit.

Row 2 (RS): With B, k1, *[sl 1 wyib, k2tog] twice, sl 1, k2; rep from *, at the end sl 1, k2tog, sl 1 wyib, k1—152 (161) sts.

Row 3: With B, k1, sl 1 wyif, p1, sl 1 wyif, p2, *[sl 1 wyif, p1] twice, sl 1 wyif, p2; rep from *, end [sl 1 wyif, p1] three times.

Row 4: Sl 1, with A p1, *[with B k1, with A p1] twice, with B k1, with A p2; rep from *, end with B k1, with A p1, with B k1.

Row 5: Sl 1, with A k1, with B p1, with A k1, with B p2, *[with A k1, with B p1] twice, with A k1, with B p2; rep from *, end [with A k1, with B p1] twice, with A k1.

Rep rows 4 & 5 three more times.

BODY SHAPING:

- -

NOTE: Slip the 1st st of each row.

- -

With A, work in rev St st as follows:

Work 32 (41, 43) sts, PM, work 61 (70, 75) sts, PM, work last 32 (41, 43) sts.

Work in rev St st for 2 more rows. On the next WS row start increases:

Work to the 1st marker, M1, slip marker, k1, M1, work to 1 st before the 2nd marker, M1, k1, slip marker, M1, knit to end—129 (156, 165) sts.

Continue working in rev St st, repeating increases every 8th row twice more—137 (164, 173) sts.

On the following 8th row, decrease/increase as follows: Sl 1, k2tog, work to the 1st marker, M1, slip marker, k1, M1, work to 1 st before the 2nd marker, M1, k1, slip marker, M1, knit to last 3 sts, k2tog, k1—139 (166, 175) sts.

Continue working in rev St st, repeating decrease/increase row on every 10th row twice more—143 (170, 179) sts.

On the following 10th row: Sl 1, k2tog, knit to last 3 sts, k2tog, k1—141 (168, 177) sts.

Work even until piece measures 17 (18, 19)"/43 (46, 48)cm from beg.

ARMHOLE SHAPING:

Work to 3 sts before the 1st marker, BO 6 sts, work to 3 sts before the 2nd marker, BO 6 sts, work to end—31 (40, 42) sts for each front and 67 (76, 81) sts for the back. Work on Left Front sts only, place remaining sts on hold.

LEFT FRONT:

Row 1 (WS): Knit to last 2 sts, k2tog—30 (39, 41) sts.

Row 2: BO 2 sts, work to end—28 (37, 39) sts.

Row 3: Rep row 1.

Row 4: BO 1, work to end—26 (35, 37) sts.

Rows 5, 6, 7, 8, & 9: Work in rev St st.

Row 10: Sl 1, p2tog, work to last 3 sts, ssp, k1—24 (33, 35) sts.

Continue working in rev St st.

On the following 4th row: Sl 1, p2tog, work to the end—23 (32, 34) sts.

On the following 4th row: Rep row 10—21(30, 32) sts.

Work in rev St st, rep row 10 every 10th row twice more—17 (26, 28) sts.

Then rep row 10 every other row 6 (8, 9) times—5 (10, 10) sts.

BO.

BACK:

Place held back sts on needles.

Rows 1 (RS) & 2: BO 2 sts, work to last 2 sts, p2tog—61 (70, 75) sts.

Rows 3 & 4: BO 1, work to end—59 (68, 73) sts.

Rows 5, 6, 7, 8, & 9: Work in rev St st.

Row 10: Sl 1, k2tog, work to last 3 sts, ssk, k1—57 (66, 71) sts.

Work in rev St st, rep row 10 on every following 4th row twice, then every 10th row twice more—49 (58, 63) sts.

Then rep row 10 every other row 8 (10, 11) times—33 (38, 41) sts.

BO.

RIGHT FRONT:

Place held sts on needle, join yarn to RS of work.

Row 1 (RS): Purl to last 2 sts, p2tog—30 (39, 41) sts.

Row 2: BO 2 sts, work to end—28 (37, 39) sts.

Row 3: Rep row 1.

Row 4: BO 1, work to end—26 (35, 37) sts.

Rows 5, 6, 7, 8, & 9: Work in rev St st.

Row 10: Sl 1, k2tog, work to last 3 sts, ssk, k1—24 (33, 35) sts.

Continue working in rev St st.

On the following 4th row: Sl 1, k2tog, work to the end—23 (32, 34) sts.

On the following 4th row: Rep row 10—21 (30, 32) sts.

Work in rev St st, rep row 10 every 10th row twice more—17 (26, 28) sts.

Then rep row 10 every other row 6 (8, 9) times—5 (10, 10) sts.

BO.

Incorporating the honeycomb pattern into a sweater was quite a challenge. As a designer, you never want your pieces to look over-worked, so I felt that little touches of the texture were just enough. I also wanted to make the pattern functional, not just decorative. In this cardigan, the scallops stop decreasing right at the waist, providing a very feminine shape.

SLEEVES (MAKE 2)

Using A, CO 51 (57, 63) sts.

Row 1 (WS): With A, knit.

Row 2 (RS): With B, k1, *sl 1 wyib, k2, turn; sl 1 wyif, p1, turn; sl 1 wyib, k1; rep from *, end sl 1 wyib, k1.

Row 3: With B, k1,*sl 1 wyif, p2; rep from *, end sl 1 wyif, p1.

Row 4: With A, k1, *k1 tbl, k2; rep from *, end k1 tbl, k1.

Next pattern repeat (decreases):

Row 1 (WS): With A, knit.

Row 2 (RS): With B, k1, *sl 1 wyib, k2tog; rep from *, end sl 1 wyib, k1—35 (39, 43) sts.

Row 3: With B, k1, *sl 1 wyif, p1; rep from *, end sl 1 wyif, p1.

Row 4: Sl 1, with A p1, *with B k1, with A p1; rep from *, end with B k1.

Row 5: Sl 1, with A k1, *with B p1, with A k1; rep from *, end with A k1.

Rep rows 4 & 5 until cuff measures 3¼"/8.5cm.

Next RS row: With B, start working in St st.

Inc 1 st at each end of every 6th row 9 (10, 11) times—53 (59, 65) sts.

Work even until sleeve measures 20 (20½, 21)"/51 (52, 53)cm from beg, ending with a WS row.

CAP SHAPING:

Rows 1 (RS) & 2: BO 3 sts, work to end.

Rows 3 & 4: BO 2 sts, work to end.

Rows 5 & 6: BO 1 st, work to end—41 (47, 53) sts.

Dec 1 st at each end on every following 6th (4th, 4th) row 4 (6, 8) times—33 (35, 37) sts.

Work dec row every other row 8 times—17 (19, 21) sts.

Work in St st for 4 (6, 4) more rows. BO.

FINISHING

Attach and sew in sleeves. Sew sleeve seams.

Using A and crochet hook, with RS facing, work sc along Left Front edge.

Row 2: Sl st in first 3 sts, sc to last 3 sts.

Rows 3 & 4: Rep row 2. Fasten off.

Rep for Right Front.

Work 1 row of sc around raglan sleeve and back neck opening. Fasten off. Weave in ends.

Weave ribbon through sts at waist, just above Honeycomb pattern.

abbreviations

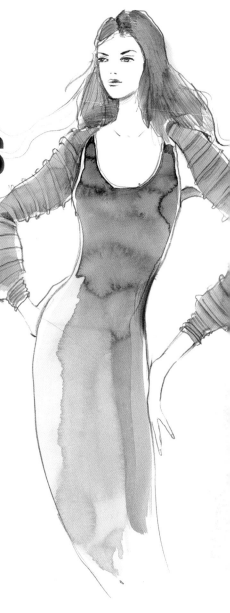

beg	begin(ning)	**R**	right
BO	bind off	**RC**	right cable
C	cable	**rem**	remaining
ch(s)	chain(s)	**rep**	repeat
cn	cable needle	**Rib**	ribbing
CO	cast on	**RS**	right side of work
dc(s)	double crochet(s)	**sc**	single crochet
dec	decrease	**sl**	slip
dtr	double treble	**ssk**	slip, slip, knit
foll	follow(ing)	**ssp**	slip, slip, purl
g-st	gathering st	**st(s)**	stitch(es)
inc	increase	**tbl**	through back loop
K or k	knit	**tog**	together
L	left	**tr**	treble
LC	left cable	**TW**	twist
MB	make bobble	**TWL**	twist left
MI	make one	**TWR**	twist right
MIB	make one with bobble	**WS**	wrong side of work
MIp	make one purl	**wyib**	with yarn in back
P or p	purl	**wyif**	with yarn in front
Pat	pattern	**yo**	yarn over
PM	place marker	**()**	work directions as a group
psso	pass slip stitch over	*****	starting point for repeated directions

YARN WEIGHT SYMBOL & CATEGORY NAMES	0 lace	1 super fine	2 fine	3 light	4 medium	5 bulky	6 super bulky
TYPE OF YARNS IN CATEGORY	Fingering 10-count crochet thread	Sock, Fingering, Baby	Sport, Baby	DK, Light Worsted	Worsted, Afghan, Aran	Chunky, Craft, Rug	Bulky, Roving

Source: Craft Yarn Council of America's www.YarnStandards.com

About the Author

Laura Zukaite moved to the United States from Lithuania when she was 18 years old. A recent graduate of Parsons School of Design, she has published designs in some of the major knitting magazines and collective designer books. *Luxe Knits* is Laura's first solo book and represents her design philosophy and creative process. Laura is currently pursuing her career as a sweater designer in New York City.

Acknowledgments

I would like to thank my mother Angelina, who is an excellent knitter, for her tremendous help in the knitting process of this book.

I am very grateful to my family, my friends Karina and Kevin Platt, Iris Schreier from Artyarns, Laurie Thomas, and the entire Sticks & Strings crew, for believing in me and supplying moral support.

Special thanks to Artyarns, the Alpaca Yarn Company, Blue Sky Alpacas, Classic Elite Yarns, Claudia Hand Painted Yarns, Jade Sapphire, and Lorna's Laces for providing the wonderful yarns for this book. Working with these luxurious yarns was a truly great experience.

Many thanks to my technical editor, Amy Polcyn, for all the smart solutions and cooperation, and to the wonderful Lark Books team: Nicole McConville, Valerie Shrader, Gavin Young, Linda Kopp, Dana Irwin, Carol Morse, and everyone else who helped to make this book come alive.

Thank you all.

About the Photographer

Cathrine Westergaard is a native New Yorker, born to a theater and film producer. Cathrine has worked for fashion magazines and record labels and has photographed celebrities as well. She was chosen as a semi-finalist for the Hasselblad Masters competition, for which she received a certificate in honor of outstanding creative and technical achievement. Cathrine resides in New York City with her son, Jaeden.

We're excited to feature the talented work of Claire Unabia and Naima Mora, who were seen on America's Next Top Model. You can see Claire Unabia on page 18 and Naima Mora on page 24.

schematics

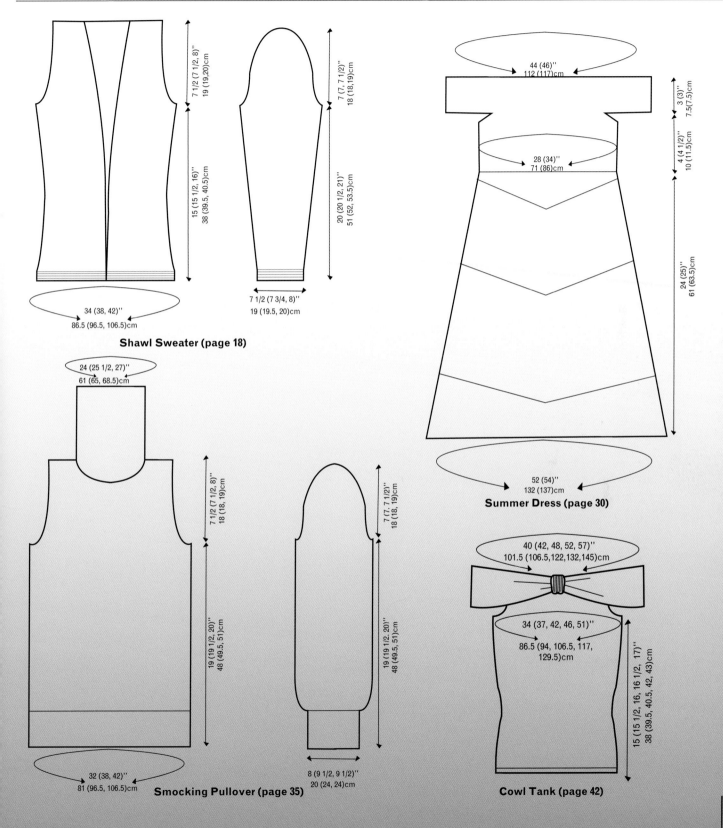

Shawl Sweater (page 18)

7 1/2 (7 1/2, 8)''
19 (19,20)cm

15 (15 1/2, 16)''
38 (39.5, 40.5)cm

34 (38, 42)''
86.5 (96.5, 106.5)cm

7 (7, 7 1/2)''
18 (18, 19)cm

20 (20 1/2, 21)''
51 (52, 53.5)cm

7 1/2 (7 3/4, 8)''
19 (19.5, 20)cm

Summer Dress (page 30)

44 (46)''
112 (117)cm

28 (34)''
71 (86)cm

3 (3)''
7.5(7.5)cm

4 (4 1/2)''
10 (11.5)cm

24 (25)''
61 (63.5)cm

52 (54)''
132 (137)cm

Smocking Pullover (page 35)

24 (25 1/2, 27)''
61 (65, 68.5)cm

7 1/2 (7 1/2, 8)''
18 (18, 19)cm

19 (19 1/2, 20)''
48 (49.5, 51)cm

32 (38, 42)''
81 (96.5, 106.5)cm

7 (7, 7 1/2)''
18 (18, 19)cm

19 (19 1/2, 20)''
48 (49.5, 51)cm

8 (9 1/2, 9 1/2)''
20 (24, 24)cm

Cowl Tank (page 42)

40 (42, 48, 52, 57)''
101.5 (106.5,122,132,145)cm

34 (37, 42, 46, 51)''
86.5 (94, 106.5, 117, 129.5)cm

15 (15 1/2, 16, 16 1/2, 17)''
38 (39.5, 40.5, 42, 43)cm

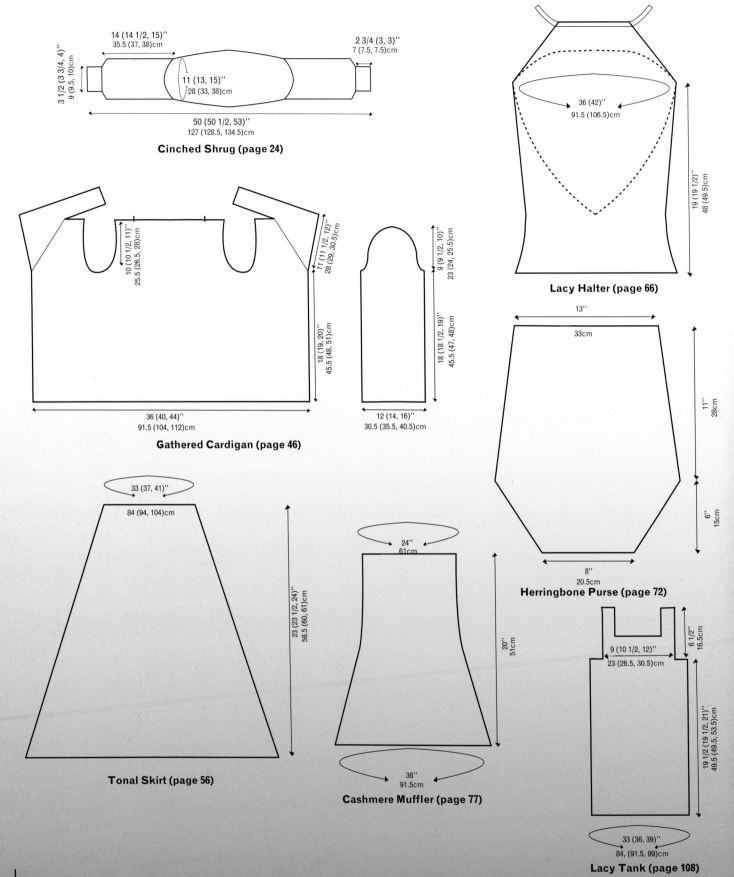

14 (14 1/2, 15)''
35.5 (37, 38)cm

2 3/4 (3, 3)''
7 (7.5, 7.5)cm

3 1/2 (3 3/4, 4)''
9 (9.5, 10)cm

11 (13, 15)''
28 (33, 38)cm

50 (50 1/2, 53)''
127 (128.5, 134.5)cm

Cinched Shrug (page 24)

36 (42)''
91.5 (106.5)cm

19 (19 1/2)''
48 (49.5)cm

Lacy Halter (page 66)

10 (10 1/2, 11)''
25.5 (26.5, 28)cm

11 (11 1/2, 12)''
28 (29, 30.5)cm

18 (19, 20)''
45.5 (48, 51)cm

9 (9 1/2, 10)''
23 (24, 25.5)cm

18 (18 1/2, 19)''
45.5 (47, 48)cm

36 (40, 44)''
91.5 (104, 112)cm

12 (14, 16)''
30.5 (35.5, 40.5)cm

Gathered Cardigan (page 46)

13''
33cm

11''
28cm

6''
15cm

8''
20.5cm

Herringbone Purse (page 72)

33 (37, 41)''
84 (94, 104)cm

23 (23 1/2, 24)''
58.5 (60, 61)cm

Tonal Skirt (page 56)

24''
61cm

20''
51cm

36''
91.5cm

Cashmere Muffler (page 77)

9 (10 1/2, 12)''
23 (26.5, 30.5)cm

6 1/2''
16.5cm

19 1/2 (19 1/2, 21)''
49.5 (49.5, 53.5)cm

33 (36, 39)''
84, (91.5, 99)cm

Lacy Tank (page 108)

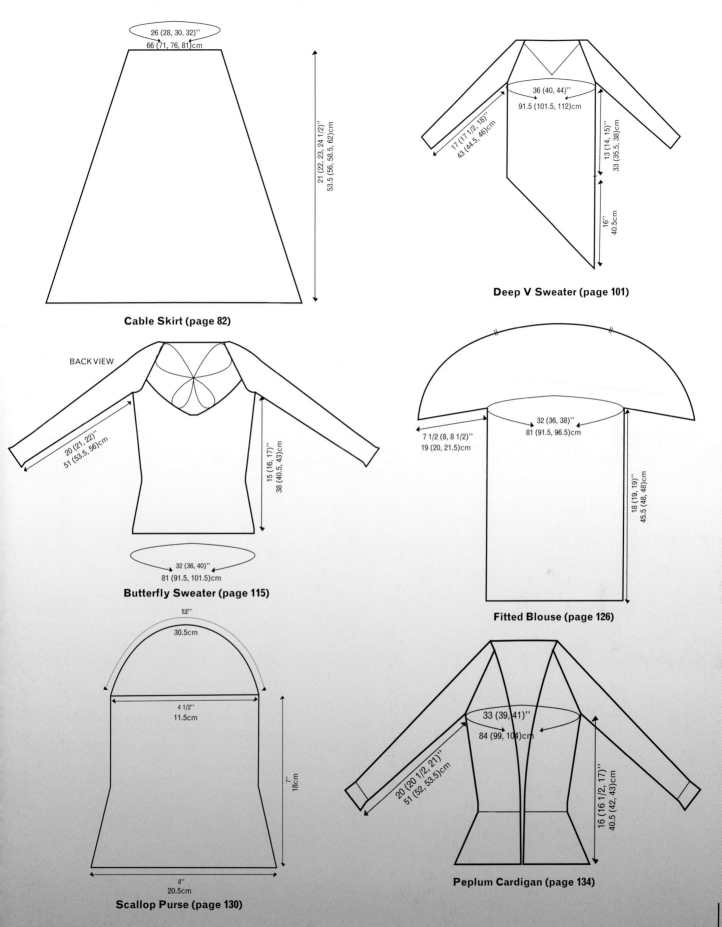

26 (28, 30, 32)''
66 (71, 76, 81)cm

21 (22, 23, 24 1/2)''
53.5 (56, 58.5, 62)cm

Cable Skirt (page 82)

36 (40, 44)''
91.5 (101.5, 112)cm

17 (17 1/2, 18)''
43 (44.5, 46)cm

13 (14, 15)''
33 (35.5, 38)cm

16''
40.5cm

Deep V Sweater (page 101)

BACK VIEW

20 (21, 22)''
51 (53.5, 56)cm

15 (16, 17)''
38 (40.5, 43)cm

32 (36, 40)''
81 (91.5, 101.5)cm

Butterfly Sweater (page 115)

32 (36, 38)''
81 (91.5, 96.5)cm

7 1/2 (8, 8 1/2)''
19 (20, 21.5)cm

18 (19, 19)''
45.5 (48, 48)cm

Fitted Blouse (page 126)

12''
30.5cm

4 1/2''
11.5cm

7''
18cm

8''
20.5cm

Scallop Purse (page 130)

33 (39, 41)''
84 (99, 104)cm

20 (20 1/2, 21)''
51 (52, 53.5)cm

16 (16 1/2, 17)''
40.5 (42, 43)cm

Peplum Cardigan (page 134)

index